ENGLAND'S HERITAGE FOOD AND COOKING

ENGLAND'S HERITAGE FOOD AND COOKING

A classic collection of 160 traditional recipes
from this rich and varied culinary landscape,
shown in 750 beautiful photographs, including
easy step-by-step sequences throughout

ANNETTE YATES

LORENZ BOOKS

This edition is published by Lorenz Books, an imprint of Anness Publishing Ltd, Hermes House, 88–89 Blackfriars Road, London SE1 8HA; tel. 020 7401 2077; fax 020 7633 9499

www.lorenzbooks.com; www.annesspublishing.com

If you like the images in this book and would like to investigate using them for publishing, promotions or advertising, please visit our website www.practicalpictures.com for more information.

UK agent: The Manning Partnership Ltd; tel. 01225 478444; fax 01225 478440; sales@manning-partnership.co.uk
UK distributor: Grantham Book Services Ltd; tel. 01476 541080; fax 01476 541061; orders@gbs.tbs-ltd.co.uk
North American agent/distributor: National Book Network; tel. 301 459 3366; fax 301 429 5746; www.nbnbooks.com
Australian agent/distributor: Pan Macmillan Australia; tel. 1300 135 113; fax 1300 135 103; customer.service@macmillan.com.au
New Zealand agent/distributor: David Bateman Ltd; tel. (09) 415 7664; fax (09) 415 8892

Publisher: Joanna Lorenz
Editorial Director: Helen Sudell
Executive Editor: Joanne Rippin
Designer: Nigel Partridge, Jacket design: Adelle Morris
Photographer: Craig Robertson
Food preparation and food styling: Fergal Connelly
Styling and props: Helen Trent
Production Controller: Lee Sargent

ETHICAL TRADING POLICY

At Anness Publishing we believe that business should be conducted in an ethical and ecologically sustainable way, with respect for the environment and a proper regard to the replacement of the natural resources we employ.

As a publisher, we use a lot of wood pulp to make high-quality paper for printing, and that wood commonly comes from spruce trees. We are therefore currently growing more than 500,000 trees in two Scottish forest plantations near Aberdeen – Berrymoss (130 hectares/320 acres) and West Touxhill (125 hectares/305 acres). The forests we manage contain twice the number of trees employed each year in paper-making for our books.

Because of this ongoing ecological investment programme, you, as our customer, can have the pleasure and reassurance of knowing that a tree is being cultivated on your behalf to naturally replace the materials used to make the book you are holding.

Our forestry programme is run in accordance with the UK Woodland Assurance Scheme (UKWAS) and will be certified by the internationally recognized Forest Stewardship Council (FSC). The FSC is a non-government organization dedicated to promoting responsible management of the world's forests. Certification ensures forests are managed in an environmentally sustainable and socially responsible basis. For further information about this scheme, go to www.annesspublishing.com/trees.

A CIP catalogue record for this book is available from the British Library.

NOTES

Bracketed terms are intended for American readers.

For all recipes, quantities are given in both metric and imperial measures and, where appropriate, in standard cups and spoons. Follow one set of measures, but not a mixture, because they are not interchangeable.

Standard spoon and cup measures are level. 1 tsp = 5ml, 1 tbsp = 15ml, 1 cup = 250ml/8fl oz.

Australian standard tablespoons are 20ml. Australian readers should use 3 tsp in place of 1 tbsp for measuring small quantities.

American pints are 16fl oz/2 cups. American readers should use 20fl oz/2.5 cups in place of 1 pint when measuring liquids.

The nutritional analysis given for each recipe is calculated per portion (i.e. serving or item), unless otherwise stated. If the recipe gives a range, such as Serves 4–6, then the nutritional analysis will be for the smaller portion size, i.e. 6 servings. Measurements for sodium do not include salt added to taste.

Medium (US large) eggs are used unless otherwise stated.

CONTENTS

Introduction

The food of England has a history that stretches back more than six thousand years, beginning with the herding and subsistence farming of the Celts, who borrowed and adapted the ideas of trading partners, importing ingredients and ideas from mainland Europe and beyond. Since then the English diet has been influenced not only by the landscape but also by invasion and immigration, a global empire, social development, trade and technology, politics and, of course, fashion.

For all the richness of England's culinary heritage and the excellence of its ingredients, for much of the 20th century it had a reputation for food that was plain and boring, consisting mainly of overcooked meat and vegetables and stodgy puddings. This decline in English food probably began in the 19th century, as Victorian morality inculcated a disdain for the sensory pleasure of eating, and the increasingly urbanized population lost touch with fresh produce. The emerging middle classes, locked between the wealthy and the poor, strove to keep up appearances with grandiose but badly cooked meals, inspired by the publication of Mrs Beeton's cookery book. A "below stairs" attitude to cooks, two World Wars, food rationing, hardship and the rise of processed foods all took their toll, and recovery from this adverse perception of English cooking has taken a long time, but today England is once more able to take pride in its reputation for excellent food.

This beautiful book begins with an overview of the country's rich food history. Along the way it considers the medieval period, when extreme poverty sat uneasily alongside the extravagance of the wealthy, the political upheaval of the 17th century, the Industrial Revolution and modern technological advances. It takes a look at the regions of England, festivals and customs and the food associated with them. But the major part of this book is devoted to cooking, with a host of delicious recipes to suit every occasion and everything you need to know about the best of English food and cooking. Enjoy it and eat well.

The history of eating in England

The food cultivation and eating traditions of England have been shaped partly by the temperate climate and geography of the British Isles, but also by the nation's history of invasion, settlement and immigration. The English are fortunate to have had a stream of foreign influences to enrich their culinary development, initially from the European mainland, but also from the Americas, Asia and the Far East.

Early times

In the days of the hunter-gatherers, before farming began, England was mostly covered by woodland. In the clearings, where trees had fallen or died, edible weeds and plants grew – including barberries, blackberries, crab apples, haws, hazelnuts and sloes. The woods were home to wild cattle, boar, cats, deer and elk, badgers, hedgehogs, shrews and other small mammals. The rivers and coastal waters were rich with fish and shellfish.

Below The Romans bought sophisticated fishing equipment to Britain, as well as elaborate fish sauces.

Prehistoric pottery was made from coarse clay and shaped into crude vessels. Some pots were porous, and were used for storage, while others could withstand the sudden and intense heat of an open fire during cooking.

The shift to farming from around 4000BC led to the growth of larger, settled communities. Livestock remained all-important until the Bronze Age (c 2000BC), from which time the first remains of grain crops and field systems date. In the Iron Age the Celts made the first metal cauldrons for cooking.

Above A reconstruction of a Celtic Iron Age village, when England was a country divided into tribes and regions.

New foods from the Romans

When the Romans arrived in England in 55BC, simple meat and vegetable stews were the order of the day. The far more sophisticated Romans were to have a huge and long-lasting influence on English eating, as they introduced a large range of foods and flavours, elaborately seasoned dishes and specialized cooking methods such as roasting and baking.

The Romans brought pheasants, peacocks and guinea fowl, and they imported a host of vegetables, including asparagus, cabbage, carrots, celery, cucumber, endive, globe artichokes, leek, marrow, onion, parsnip, turnip, radish and shallots. There were herbs such as borage, chervil, coriander, dill, fennel, mint, parsley, thyme, rosemary, sage, savory and sweet marjoram. Spices included cinnamon, ginger and pepper, and there were almonds, dates, olives, olive oil, pine kernels, walnuts and wine – the customary drink of Roman soldiers. They also introduced orchard trees such as damson, cherry, medlar, mulberry and plum. As well as importing dried grapes in the form of

raisins and sultanas, they established vines, using the grapes to make wine for drinking, must for cooking and vinegar for drinks, sauces and preserving. The Romans also brought their favourite fermented fish sauces, called *liquamen* and *garum* (similar to South-east Asian fish sauces, and the forerunners of modern concoctions such as Worcestershire sauce), which they used in savoury and sweet dishes.

The Romans held extravagant banquets featuring foods that now sound outlandish, such as milk-fattened snails, stuffed dormice and wild boar stuffed with live birds. Most notoriously, some of them indulged in the habit of inducing vomiting after eating several courses of rich food before coming back for more.

Farming practices also changed with the Romans, who created hare gardens and game parks for red, roe and fallow deer. Beef was popular and cattle also provided milk, butter and cheese. Pigs were plentiful and ham was salted (with sea salt) or pickled in brine. Sheep and goats were kept for meat, and their milk was made into cheeses. The Romans also kept hens and honey bees. Oysters were highly prized and came from England's south-east coast. Wheat and cereal grains were made into porridge and gruel as well as being used in baking. Flour was mainly ground at home by hand, using a rotary quern, though it has been confirmed that commercial bakeries existed in large towns and that the Romans made a variety of breads.

Anglo-Saxons and Vikings

The Anglo-Saxons – Germanic tribes who settled in England from the 5th century following the fall of the Roman Empire – ate what they grew. Their cereals included wheat and rye for bread, barley for brewing and oats for porridge and animal food. There were

Above *After the chaos of invasion and settlement, Danish invaders to England introduced new food and customs.*

vegetables (beans, cabbages, carrots, parsnip, peas and onions) and fruit (apples, cherries and plums).

Meat was in fairly short supply. Though wild animals such as deer and wild boar were common, only landowners had the right to kill them. Pigs were the only animals kept solely for their meat – they produced large litters, which matured quickly in readiness for slaughter. Sheep provided wool as well as meat, while cows produced milk, meat, hides and glue.

The Anglo-Saxons also ate fish, from both rivers and the sea. Everyone, even the children, drank weak ale, which was safer than the water from wells, streams and rivers. Wine was imported from the continent but was drunk only by the wealthy. Other options were buttermilk and whey (by-products from butter and cheese-making), with mead for special occasions.

The Viking invaders of the 8th and 9th centuries also influenced eating habits in England. These new settlers were proud of their hospitality, and willingly shared their homes and food with strangers. They ate a wide variety of fruits, nuts and grains, as well as fish and shellfish. Meat was available to all, not just reserved for the rich, and game animals included hare, boar, deer, squirrel and wild birds.

Dairy products formed an important part of the Viking diet, with whole milk reserved for butter-making. Eggs were supplied by chickens, geese, ducks and wild birds (gulls' eggs were a special delicacy). Fish and meat were preserved for the winter months by salting, pickling, drying or smoking. Bread – both leavened and unleavened – was made in large quantities, and the Vikings made use of wild yeasts and raising agents such as buttermilk, sour milk and yeast left over from brewing. The bread was often flavoured with nuts, seeds, herbs or cheese, or used to wrap fish or meat.

Medieval extremes

What people ate varied according to social standing in the medieval period, as did their place at the table. Most still prepared their own food, or traded it with others. Though some food shops were to be found in towns, most people were peasants living in villages, where there were no traders. Potting and drying were popular ways of preserving food, and salt was an important ingredient, kept dry in a box by the fire.

In the Middle Ages bread was the staple food of all classes, though only rich farmers and lords ate white bread, for they were able to grow wheat, which required well-dug and manured soil. The most common bread, called "maslin", was coarse and made with a mixture of wheat and rye. Rye and barley breads were heavy and dark and were eaten only by the poorest. Feudal laws often meant that peasants were not allowed to bake bread in their own huts by the central fire, but had to take their dough to the manor for baking, where they were obliged to give up a proportion to feed the lord's servants. At the medieval table, bread was used

to make trenchers – rough plate shapes cut from stale loaves – which were not eaten by the diners, but might be offered to beggars or animals at the end of the meal.

Pottage, a soupy mixture of vegetables, meat, pulses, cereals, herbs and broth, was eaten by everyone every day and was cooked in the basic utensil of the time – the cauldron. This was a three-legged cast-iron pot that stood or hung over the open fire.

Fish was very important in the diet too. The population at that time belonged to the Roman Catholic Church, which meant many days in the year when meat, eggs or dairy foods were forbidden, so fish would be eaten instead. A huge herring industry existed in England and most people ate salted or pickled herrings round the year. Only landowners and the rich had a wider choice of fresh fish and shellfish, though villagers were sometimes granted permission to catch certain fish from local rivers.

Cattle, sheep and goats provided meat, but the mainstay of the poor was the pig. Pigs could forage for their own

food, could be slaughtered at any time of year, and were suitable for sausage-making and for smoking and salting in readiness for winter consumption. Though game animals roamed in the woodland surrounding most villages, they remained the privilege of the wealthy and the property of kings and nobles. Poachers faced mutilation or death, though many peasants did get permission to hunt hares, rabbits, hedgehogs and squirrels.

The main drink of medieval days was ale, though villagers were not allowed to sell it without permission and a paid-for licence from their lord.

Cooked dishes for the wealthy were flavoured with expensive imported spices such as cardamom, caraway, ginger, nutmeg and pepper, and foods were dyed with vivid natural colourings such as sandalwood, saffron and boiled blood. There were other exotic imports such as sugar, citrus fruits, dried fruits and almonds – all treasured by the wealthy. Medieval banquets would have spectacular centrepieces such as roasted swans or peacocks complete with plumage, or lavish sugar sculptures.

Left *A medieval banquet, such as this one where the dukes of York, Gloucester and Ireland dine with King Richard II, was a chance for the host to display his power, wealth and position.*

Class distinctions

The numerous French words that entered the English language following the Norman Conquest included the names of the meats that were eaten by the Norman aristocracy, such as mutton, beef, veal and pork. Meanwhile the old Anglo-Saxon names – sheep, cow and pig – continued to be used for the live animals, as they were tended by the English peasants.

Above Ladies of the court dressed in their finery parade a peacock re-dressed in his, for a banquet's centrepiece.

Tudor England

The Tudor period was a time of colour, splendour, pomp and ceremony. While the English nobility had a reputation for overeating, even the lower classes ate well compared with most of their European counterparts.

At the table, trenchers (plates) began to be made of wood rather than bread, but the foods that were enjoyed were similar to those of the Middle Ages, with bread, pottage, fish and meat underpinning the diet. Vegetables and fruit were treated with suspicion and left for the lower classes. They were often thought to be responsible for sickness and disease – during the plague of 1569, for example, the selling of fresh fruit became illegal. As a result, vitamin deficiencies were common.

Meanwhile, expeditions to the New World were bringing back new and exotic foods for the enjoyment of the rich: potatoes, tomatoes, maize, chocolate, peanuts, pepper, pineapples, tapioca, turkey and vanilla. From southern Europe came apricots, blackcurrants, lemons, oranges, melons, pomegranates, quinces, raspberries and

redcurrants, all of which the wealthy attempted to grow in the gardens of their large houses.

Sugar, though still expensive, had become more widely available and was very popular with the wealthy – so much so that their teeth were often decayed, as were those of Queen Elizabeth I. A refinery was built in London and sugar was sold in large cone-shaped lumps that required grating or pounding before use. It was added to meat, fish and vegetable

dishes as well as being used to make syrups, preserves and sweetmeats such as marzipan and crystallized fruits.

Standards for cooking and eating were firmly set by royalty, and the palaces served enormous quantities of elaborate dishes every day. Huge kitchens were equipped with several fireplaces, with spits for roasting, and dozens of bronze pots and pans. They required large storage areas for food, ale, beer and wine, spacious bakehouses and extensive kitchen gardens, not to mention teams of domestic staff. This theme was replicated on a smaller scale, in the large country houses of the major landowners. Whereas in the early medieval house the lord and his family had eaten in the great hall with all his retainers, private dining chambers now came into use. Sumptuous feasts were the order of the day, providing the aristocracy with the opportunity to display their wealth and manners.

Below A wonderful picture of a kitchen in Tudor times, with its cavernous fires, and foodstuffs hung high on the walls.

Centuries of upheaval

The 17th century was an era of political turmoil in England, and also saw enormous changes in food and eating. The dissolution of the monasteries in the previous century had created a new class of non-aristocratic landowner – the landed gentry, as they were to become known.

It became fashionable for this affluent new class to visit towns, and London became the finest source of both social graces and luxury foods. While most of the foodstuffs we know today had already been introduced, the arrival of allspice, cochineal, sago, tea, coffee and chocolate caused great excitement. Coffee houses opened, first in Oxford and then in London. Interest in foreign foods and new cooking methods continued to grow. Standards were still set by the royal household, with much of its influence drawn from France, and (fancy) French cuisine gained mass popularity. Fresh fruit and vegetables were now considered safe to eat and diners began to appreciate salads.

At the same time, the English continued to enjoy their traditional foods, with meat forming a large part of the diet. Baking skills improved greatly, as local specialities were developed in the form of cakes,

biscuits, buns and pastries. The traditional English pudding was born with the invention of the pudding cloth, a square of muslin (cheesecloth) in which the ball of dough was tied and cooked slowly in a pot with the meat and vegetables. There were oven-baked puddings too, based on rice or eggs.

Every country house, no matter how modest, had a kitchen garden. Those on large country estates boasted raised beds, hot beds and hothouses, all of which produced a huge range of vegetables and fruit. Icehouses were

Above *The interior of an early London coffee house, c.1705, where customers were exclusively male.*

built to store winter ice for cooling food and drink in summer, and ice cream began to be made.

Beehive ovens and stoves appeared alongside the kitchen fireplaces in large

Below *By the 1600s English country houses had kitchen gardens on their estates, and established rooms inside that were specifically for dining.*

houses, and an early pressure cooker, the "steam digester", was invented in 1679. Ladies began to exchange recipes at parties and compile recipe books. Meals were served buffet style (with a range of dishes offered at the same time) and eating took place in the "dining room".

Georgian progress

In the early 1700s, the English people were still growing and rearing their own food and eating off the land. But landowners began to enclose their land, driving off the peasants (who lost their homes as well as their vegetable plots), to free it up for commercial farming. As a result the poor struggled to survive, moving to towns and cities to work in the new factories, living in slums (particularly in the Midlands and the south of England), and eating a diet of bread, potatoes and porridge. Town life throbbed with activity: shops, markets, cattle traffic, puppet shows, dog fights, fops, prostitutes and pickpockets all packed the streets. It was an age of gambling on both a large scale (on the stock market) and a small scale (in domino games or cockfighting). Spirits, such as gin, were cheap and drunkenness was rife among the poor – men, women and children.

Much more meat was available (and cheap to buy) as a result of new winter feeding practices for livestock, land enclosure and better breeding methods. Improved transport meant that regional foods like cheeses, fresh fish and oysters (which were plentiful) could be transported throughout the country. Sugar was now readily available, and replaced spices and herbs to make food palatable, leading to the development of pickles, ketchups and bottled sauces. Sugar was also added to drinks – wine, tea, coffee and chocolate. Coffee and tea were still expensive treats for the wealthy (China tea was kept in a locked caddy to stop the servants drinking it), and smuggling was prevalent. But tea's popularity exploded in England in the early 18th century. Between breakfast (of bread, beef and ale) and dinner at the end of the day there was a long gap, and to fill it the Georgians began to take afternoon tea, displaying their wealth in ornate teapots and tea sets.

By the mid-18th century the dinner table looked much as it does today, with plates, bowls, knives, forks, serving spoons and wine glasses. Etiquette became important – not eating too quickly or too slowly, not sitting too close or too distant from the table, and no scratching or spitting.

Although the aristocracy employed French chefs, the swelling ranks of middle England enjoyed simple, plain fare such as roast and boiled meats and pies. Rebelling against fancy French sauces, the English became known for their preference for plain roast beef, and their love affair with puddings really took hold. A huge variety was enjoyed – boiled, baked, stuffed with meat or game – and most were loaded with butter or suet. In fact, butter, though twice the cost of meat, was used copiously in most dishes.

This age of indulgence led to widespread health problems, with a high incidence of gout, diabetes, heart and liver diseases, and vitamin deficiencies. Many foods were secretly or unwittingly made with poisonous ingredients. Copper and lead were used to make pickles green, sweets multicoloured, and cheese rind red. Pepper was mixed with floor sweepings to bulk it out, and alum (a toxic mineral salt) was added to bread to whiten it. Copper and brass pans, when used to cook acidic food, produced a poisonous layer of verdigris. Perhaps as a result of all this, towards the end of the century spa towns became fashionable as people tried to improve their health.

Below *By the 18th century dinner parties were elaborate, and formal occasions with new etiquette, manners and customs were well established.*

The Victorian age and beyond

The reign of Queen Victoria was a time of burgeoning industrial development, during which the gap between rich and poor widened even further, and poverty and plenty sat side by side. It was a time of factories, railways, pollution, gadgets, extravagance, mass poverty, starvation, destitution and charity; a time of poor harvests, crop diseases, famine and food riots. The growing population continued to move from the country to the city in search of work, with the poor supplying cheap labour for the factories and the growing middle classes holding high-status jobs. For some, life became so difficult that it prompted a humanitarian movement that offered charity in the hardest-hit areas. There were even cookery books directed at feeding the poor.

The invention of the steam engine improved transportation of fresh foodstuffs such as milk and other dairy produce, fish and meat. Meanwhile, the discovery of bacteria led to advances in medicine and food preservation, and to a greater awareness of food hygiene. As a result, the quality of produce in the cities improved, and international trade also took off.

Below Billingsgate Market in 1861, a large fish market in London that still exists today, in a different location.

With more tea and wheat in England than ever before, prices dropped. Tea had been a valuable delicacy in the previous century; now it became the staple drink of the poor, who drank it in copious quantities as they ate their bread or potatoes.

The development of roller mills meant that white flour (and therefore white bread) was available to all. And the canning process, patented in 1810, meant that cheap meat could be shipped from the other side of the world and all kinds of produce – vegetables, fruit, soups, stews – could be preserved without being salted or pickled. Street food was popular in towns and cities and the first fish and chip shop opened in London in 1860.

Above An illustration of some of the popular puddings of the day, taken from Beeton's Everyday Cookery and Housekeeping Book, of 1888.

Victorian kitchens were large – able to hold the new cast-iron ranges, with their open fires, ovens, water tank and hot plate. They burned coal (wood had previously been the main fuel) and for the first time cooks were able to control the temperature in their ovens. Cooks in middle-class houses could now prepare the complicated meals and delicate dishes that had been the reserve of grand kitchens in wealthy homes. Mrs Beeton's *Book of Household Management*, published in 1861, was popular with young, middle-class families, and was followed by many other recipe books.

A battery of cast-iron and tin-plated equipment replaced brass and copper. Kitchens were filled with mass-produced equipment such as pastry cutters, baking tins, pie moulds and jelly moulds; and gadgets such as graters, potato peelers, mincers and bean slicers. There was usually a walk-in pantry to keep food cool and plenty of storage space for the vast array of packets, cans and bottles – all of which were prized by the urban middle class, who no longer grew their own food. The fishmonger, greengrocer and

milkman delivered straight to the door. In the country meanwhile, where railway lines had not yet been laid, the people continued to live off the land.

The end of the 19th century saw the introduction of gas stoves, electric kettles and facilities for chilling and freezing meat. As the production of goods increased, so did the importance of the British Empire, which provided new markets in which mass-produced goods could be sold. Consequently, vast amounts of cargo moved around the world, and the colonies became increasingly dependent on imports.

The modern age

At the beginning of the 20th century the English population ate very poorly. In 1917, when 2,500,000 men from across the social spectrum were given medical examinations, around 40 per cent of them were found to be unfit for military service – mainly due to malnourishment. Vitamins and their importance in a healthy diet had only recently been discovered, and the government now began to invest in dietary research.

After a period of recovery from World War I came the General Strike, during which soup kitchens were set up to feed communities, and a time of great depression and poverty followed. At the same time, the better off were beginning to eat out: the first Indian restaurants opened in London and the first "sit-down" fish and chip restaurant appeared in Guiseley, near Leeds. Milk was pasteurized and bottled, and sliced bread and instant coffee went on sale.

In spite of the shortages caused by the lack of imports and diversion of resources, World War II is now considered to have been a period of relatively healthy eating in England. The government introduced food rationing in 1940, with the Ministry of Food advising the nation on eating healthily

and growing their own food. Meats, fats, cheese, butter, eggs, sugar and sweets were all rationed, and the resulting diet was rich in bread, potatoes and vegetables. "Dig for Victory" posters appeared all over the country and allotments popped up on every corner. Pregnant mothers and infants were given free milk, cod liver oil and vitamins; calcium was added to flour to prevent rickets, and the National Loaf (which was brown bread) was introduced. One of the few meals not to be rationed was fish and chips, and vans toured around feeding the armed forces and evacuees.

The development of freezing, canning and freeze-drying techniques led to food technologists finding new ways to enhance and preserve foods. They created a host of chemical additives, that included flavour enhancers, anticoagulants, colours and preservatives (all of which are identified by "E-numbers"). Shoppers were able to buy food that was decalred to be convenient, but was also emulsified, homogenized, high in fat, high in salt, brightly coloured, fizzy, and fast.

Above *Wealthy Victorians enjoyed imported delicacies, better cooking equipment and complex new recipes.*

Supermarkets and fast food outlets appeared all over the country and pre-packed ready-made meals became fashionable. Faster transport by air and sea meant foods could be imported from all over the world around the year.

In the last forty years the country has seen the threat of genetically modified foods, the over-fishing of coastal waters and food scares, with chemicals banned and the egg, beef and sheep industries under investigation. Today, alongside the continued growth of supermarkets, fast foods and eating out, there are signs of a return to traditional ways. The English are beginning to question where their food comes from and how it is produced. There is increased interest in seasonal foods, organic farming and environmental issues. And there is an interest in the past for inspiration, finding the best in the heritage of English cooking and applying it to modern methods of providing good, healthy food.

England's regions: The South-east

This corner of England features chalk downs, dramatic cliffs and large seaports, and at its centre sprawls the capital city, London. In spite of its dense population the region's mild climate and warm, rich soil makes it a prime source of fresh produce, high quality meat and fish, and dairy products.

Grazing the fields

Sheep have always grazed the lowlands, and quality lamb and mutton comes from the South Downs. The Romney sheep is a pure breed that feeds on the

Below England's temperate climate and surrounding seas make it ideal land for farming and food production.

salt marsh pastures of Sussex and Kent, producing meat with a fine, distinctive flavour. Pig farms abound in Hampshire in particular, and the county hosts one of the largest sausage competitions in the country. Hampshire haslet (a pork loaf) is a local speciality.

Poultry has always been important in this area, both for eggs and for the rearing of table birds. As far back as the 1600s, the Surrey town of Dorking was said to host the greatest poultry market in England. The White Dorking chicken is famous for its unusual fifth claw and was a favourite with Queen Victoria. The Aylesbury duck, with its white plumage and orange legs and feet, is the largest of the domestic ducks and has been popular for two centuries.

***Above** The coastline along the south-east of England is still fished for shellfish such as whelks and cockles.*

Game in south-east England includes venison from the New Forest, a medieval enclave established by William the Conqueror for the preservation of deer for royal hunts, which is still largely in the possession of the Crown. In addition, pheasant, partridge and hare are shot in the region.

Historically, the area is better known for dairy farming than for beef. Until the mid-1800s Londoners were supplied with milk from herds that grazed on Clapham Common and Hampstead Heath. Though there is no ancient tradition of cheese-making, some fine farmhouse cheeses are now made in the area, such as Spenwood, Sussex Slipcote and Oxford Blue.

Coast and river

While the long Kent coastline has seen a huge decline in the fishing industry, there are still fine Dover sole and a variety of fish and shellfish to be bought direct from little huts and harbours along the seafront. In Sussex,

fishing is still an important business, and sea bass, red and grey mullet and conger eels are caught. Whitstable, on the Kent coast, has long been known as the oyster centre of England, and an annual oyster festival is still celebrated. Smokehouses and fish farms, mainly for rainbow trout, are dotted around.

The River Thames was once full of eels and its tributary the Wandle, now submerged under the streets of south London, was one of the finest trout streams. In Hampshire, the River Test still yields wild trout, pike and zander.

Market gardens

Known until recently as the "Garden of England", Kent grows much of the country's fruit. Spring blossoms promise apples (Cox's Orange Pippin and Bramley both originated in Kent), pears, plums and cherries, and the National Fruit Collections are based at Brogdale. There are soft fruits too, and cobnuts, a variety of hazelnut, are a local treat. Market gardens along the Sussex Weald produce large amounts of fruit (particularly gooseberries), vegetables and salad crops. Sussex is also known for its mushroom farms. Hampshire and the Isle of Wight produce cereals, root vegetables and watercress.

Below The famous Aylesbury duck has been a popular duck to rear for the table for over 200 years.

Hops, apples and vines

Many of the oast houses in which hops for beer-making were dried still stand in the Kent countryside. Harvest is celebrated at Faversham's hop festival. The area is dotted with breweries, and Kent and Sussex are also cider-making centres, making the most of local apples. South-facing slopes in the area are increasingly being planted with vines, following a tradition of viticulture first brought to England by the Romans.

Bakes and cakes

The Bedfordshire clanger – originally a portable midday meal for farm labourers – is a hefty suet pastry with a savoury filling at one end and a sweet one at the other.

St Clement's cake, made with butter, currants, spice, candied peel and sugar, is special to Berkshire, where until the late 1800s it was sold at the sheep fair in Lambourn on St Clement's Day (23 November). Oxfordshire has Banbury cakes (oval pastries filled with mixed dried fruit) and, since 1874, has been associated with Frank Cooper's distinctive Oxford marmalade.

Kent has its Kentish huffkins – small bread rolls made with a dimple for holding jam or cream. Flead cakes, similar to lardy cakes, were traditionally made at pig-killing time. In the Kent village of Biddenden, little cakes bearing a picture of the village's medieval Siamese twins, the Biddenden Maids, are distributed at Easter as part of an ancient charity set up by the sisters and known as the Biddenden Dole.

In Surrey, lardy cakes, also known as dough cakes or breakfast cakes, traditionally contained caraway seeds as well other spices and dried fruit. Guildford manchets are soft buttery rolls. Sussex has its lemony Sussex pond pudding and the Isle of Wight is known for its doughnuts.

Above The apple orchards of Kent grow a number of different English apple varieties.

The streets of London

Until the early 1900s, London resounded to the cries and bell ringing of street traders, such as the muffin man who came bearing a tray of fresh muffins and crumpets on his head. Well into the 20th century there were barrows selling shellfish – cockles, prawns (shrimp), winkles and whelks – roasted chestnuts are still sold in the streets around Christmas time. London's famous Chelsea buns were originally sold in the 18th century by a company called Chelsea Bun House, in Pimlico.

Since the 18th century, the East End of London has been home to eel and pie shops, selling stewed or jellied eels and meat pies. London is also famous for dishes such as whitebait (tiny fish deep-fried and eaten whole) and boiled beef and carrots. It still has pubs, chop houses and grill rooms serving English specialities such as steak and kidney pudding, and game pies. Its ancient food markets include Covent Garden, Billingsgate, and Smithfield.

The South-west

This fertile region enjoys the mildest climate in England. It remains a popular holiday destination, with thatched cottages, fishing villages, shady creeks and glorious beaches. The seas are warmed by the Gulf Stream and spring always arrives early.

Cream, cheese and butter

Rich dairy pastures produce milk with a high butterfat content – ideal for making the cream, cheese, butter and ice cream for which the region is famous. The area is probably best known for its clotted cream, which is extremely thick and yellow, with a wrinkled, grainy crust and a distinctive flavour. Clotted cream keeps well and is sent as a souvenir all over the world. Local cream teas would not be correct without it.

There are cheeses galore. From Gloucestershire, where a traditional cheese-rolling race is still held in spring, come Single and Double Gloucester, some still made with milk from the now rare Gloucester cattle. Stinking Bishop, with its perry-washed rind and potent smell, is also made with this milk. Farther south, there is Dorset Blue Vinney and, in Somerset, perhaps the most copied of English cheeses – Cheddar. Meanwhile, Devon is proud of its blue cheeses: Devon Blue from cow's milk, Beenleigh Blue from ewe's milk and Harbourne Blue from goat's milk. Cornish Yarg, a tangy, white cheese made with cows' milk, has a distinctive rind made from nettle leaves.

Vegetables and fruit

Dorset produces delicious watercress, lettuces, peas and cabbage, as well as carrots, Brussels sprouts and onions. From the famous chalk-stone cliffs come sea kale, samphire and sea holly, the root of which was once candied and thought to be an aphrodisiac.

Above *The wide estuary of Fowey, in Cornwall, still supports a successful sea-based community.*

Cornwall's warm climate produces early fruit and vegetables, including new potatoes, peas, broad beans and, from the Tamar Valley, strawberries. Gooseberries grow well there and are traditionally served with the locally caught mackerel. Apple orchards flourish throughout the region and pear orchards feature in Devon.

Coast and river

The extensive coastline is dotted with bustling harbours. In Devon, large numbers of fishing boats used to go out of Brixham, Plymouth and the tiny fishing villages where shoals of mackerel and herring were once landed. Today's catches are small, but may include haddock, mullet (red and grey), mackerel, turbot and sea bream, as well as crabs, lobsters and shellfish (scallops in particular).

Off the Cornish coast, pilchards (large sardines) were once the largest catch of the region, and they are the filling for stargazy pie, the whole fish arranged with their heads sticking out of the pastry as if gazing at the stars. Mackerel is now the main catch but at Newlyn and Falmouth monkfish, sole, hake, skate and other varieties are landed.

The River Severn is known for its salmon fishing and has been fished for elvers (baby eels) for hundreds of years: until 1990 annual elver-eating contests were held at Frampton-on-Severn.

Pigs in orchards

While there is excellent beef and early lamb from the rich inland pastures of Dorset and Devon, pig farming is the tradition of the south-west and of Wiltshire in particular. Many local food specialities are based on pork and bacon, and as always every part of the animal is utilized.

Bradenham ham has a distinctive black skin and a sweet subtle flavour, which comes from being soaked in molasses flavoured with spices and juniper berries before being smoked and matured. Bath chaps are cured pig's cheeks, traditionally from the famous Gloucester Old Spot breed, which enjoys eating windfall apples during the autumn. Bath chaps are salted, smoked, then boiled. They are served cold, or coated in breadcrumbs and fried.

Other pork dishes include sausages, pies, faggots, brawn, chitterlings and trotters. Jellied stock goes into pork pies, lard is rendered and blood goes into black puddings (blood sausages). Pork fat mixed with oatmeal is made into white puddings.

Cream teas and bakes

Cream teas are legendary in the south-west, with scones or splits (soft dough buns), strawberry jam and, of course, clotted cream. Wiltshire's lardy cake is made from white bread dough, rolled and folded with lard, sugar and dried fruit. Wiltshire fairings and Cornish fairings are similar to brandy snaps but more lace-like. They were originally sold at the town fairs, which were held for the hiring of agricultural workers.

Apple cakes are particularly popular in Dorset and Devon. Dorset knobs are crisp, roll-shaped biscuits, and Devon flats are biscuits (cookies) that are made with clotted cream.

From the Georgian city of Bath comes the Bath Oliver biscuit, developed by

Below The once rare breed Gloucester Old Spot has made a come back in Somerset in recent years.

the doctor who founded the Mineral Water Hospital in the city, the Bath bun, made with rich yeast dough topped with currants and crushed lump sugar, and the Sally Lunn, reputedly of 17th-century origin – a round, light, yeast cake, traditionally split and spread with butter or clotted cream.

There are cakes made with fruit and honey (the monks of Buckfast Abbey look after bee colonies in Devon and Cornwall and sell the honey in the Abbey shop). Spices would arrive at West Country ports from all over the

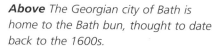

Above The Georgian city of Bath is home to the Bath bun, thought to date back to the 1600s.

world, with saffron remaining a favourite baking ingredient to this day. Last but not least is the Cornish pasty, a portable meal of meat, root vegetables and onions wrapped in thick pastry, originally designed for farmers and miners to carry to work. Authentic pasties are made with cubed, not ground, beef although legend has it that the devil would not cross the River Tamar into Cornwall for fear that the people there would put anything into their pasties.

Cider, scrumpy and gin

With apples so abundant, cider has always been, and still is the traditional drink of the region, certainly in rural areas. Traditional dry ciders are made with sour cider apples, originally crushed using a horse-drawn stone wheel. Cider made on the farm from small apples or windfalls is known as scrumpy. Plymouth has the oldest gin distillery in England, which has been supplying the Royal Navy with gin for more than 200 years.

The Midlands

This large and varied region at the heart of England is an area of valleys, rugged hills, peat bogs and moors. While it is still the home of many industries, it also has rich agricultural land, which offer orchards laden with fruit, natural spring waters and some of the best reared beef in the country.

Local meat

The ginger-haired Tamworth pig is the traditional breed in the Midlands. Pork scratchings (slivers of the crisply cooked rind) remain a local delicacy and hot roast pork rolls are a favourite. For centuries, frugal cottagers used every part of their home-reared pigs, and the legacy of this practice is the wide range of pork products that remain popular, from home-cured bacon, chitterlings, tripe and trotters to faggots, haslet, brawn, black pudding (blood sausage), sausages and pies. The most famous pork pies have been made in Melton Mowbray, Leicestershire, since the 1850s. These raised pies with their crisp hot-water-crust pastry are stuffed with chopped fresh pork and savoury jelly.

The Hereford, one of England's oldest and best-known breeds of beef cattle,

Below The beautiful Victoria plum, with its distinctive rosy blush, is grown in farms throughout Herefordshire.

A happy accident
In the 1830s the Worcester chemists Lea & Perrins tried to concoct a new spiced condiment at the request of one of their customers, but it was considered too strong to be edible and left in a barrel in the basement of their shop. When rediscovered some time later, it was found to have fermented and mellowed, and the partners bottled and sold it with great success.

dates back to the 17th century. The Derbyshire Dales are well known for sheep rearing, though sheep are farmed all over the region.

The Nottingham Goose Fair has been held in October since the 1200s. Today it is a funfair, but originally geese were brought to the fair to be sold before being herded to London.

Cheeses

A mild climate and frequent rain produces rich pastures, making the Midlands one of the country's most prolific milk-producing regions. Its abundance led to the region's fame in cheese-making, with Stilton the best known. Stilton has been popular since

the 18th century and is still made with milk exclusively from Leicestershire, Nottinghamshire and Derbyshire.

Cheshire cheese is one of the oldest English cheeses, and it has been made continuously since the 12th century. In the 17th century sage was added to Derby cheese for its alleged health-giving properties, creating Sage Derby. Shropshire Blue is a fairly modern cheese, and Red Leicester is named for its distinctive colour.

Fruits and vegetables

In the vast orchards of Worcestershire's Vale of Evesham a large variety of apples grow, and apples feature on Worcester's coat of arms. Pears grow especially well in Herefordshire, and the area around Pershore forms the centre of English plum production, with Victoria plums the most popular and Pershore Yellow Egg the most interesting. The spring blossom is a beautiful sight and organized Blossom Trails guide visitors along the scenic routes of the Vale of Evesham.

Numerous vegetables grow in the market gardens of Herefordshire and Worcestershire, and the local asparagus

Below Leicestershire's lakes and rivers are stocked with bream, carp, roach, tench and trout.

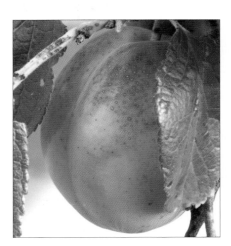

is particularly famous. Leicestershire is proud of its Brussels sprouts and the Vale of Evesham produces fine salad crops and runner beans as well as plums. There are also herb farms in this area and an increasing number of farms where vegetables are intensively grown.

Rivers and lakes

With little coastline, the area has always relied on rivers and lakes for local fish, though stocks are now severely depleted. The River Severn was formerly a rich source of salmon, eels and elvers (small eels, which were a local delicacy). The Dee and Wye are also well-known salmon-fishing rivers, with pike and grayling running in them too. There are several fish farms across the region.

Cakes and puddings

Brandy snaps and gingerbread are particularly popular and for centuries have been sold at fairs throughout the region. Staffordshire fruitcakes are enriched with treacle (molasses) and brandy, and the region is proud of its clangers – hefty pastries with either savoury or sweet fillings, similar to the Bedfordshire clanger. To the north, in Northamptonshire, the making of little cheesecakes was traditional at sheep-shearing time.

Though barley and wheat are now the main crops of the region, oats were important in the 18th and 19th centuries. Still famous are Staffordshire oatcakes, made with yeast and fine oatmeal, and resembling pancakes. Pikelets are thick, holey pancakes, traditionally served hot and oozing with melted butter at teatime.

Black Country faggots

Faggots, which used to be known as "poor man's goose" or "savoury ducks" are made from a mixture of pork offal, onion, breadcrumbs and seasoning, wrapped in caul – the lining of the pig's stomach. "Faggot" comes from the Latin word for "bundle".

Above *A view of the Peak District in Derbyshire, where sheep graze on the verdant grass of the hillsides.*

Specialities from Midland towns include crisp, lemony Shrewsbury biscuits (cookies), which have been baked there for centuries, and Bakewell puddings, which it is claimed were invented in Bakewell in the Peak District in the 1860s; the original shop is still there. Coventry godcakes, triangular in shape to represent the Holy Trinity, were often presented by godparents to their godchildren for good luck.

Orchards and springs

While the area is important for hop growing and brewing, it is far better known for its cider and perry, the latter made from the fermented juice of pears. There is also a lesser-known cider made from plums, called plum jerkum.

The area produces some famous mineral waters, from the springs of Ashbourne and Buxton in the Peak District and the Malvern Hills.

The eastern counties

This low-lying part of England facing the North Sea, with its cold winters and warm summers, is rich arable land. The area called the Fens spreads out from the Wash across Cambridgeshire, Lincolnshire and West Norfolk. Once a swampy wilderness, it was reclaimed with a network of tranquil waterways. The Norfolk and Suffolk Broads are Britain's largest protected wetland.

Fields and more fields

The soil is fertile and warm and tends to be dry, and all sorts of crops thrive. There are plenty of vegetables: Lincolnshire is especially known for its peas and early crops, while East Anglia

Below One of the characteristic windmills of the Norfolk Broads, used both for grinding corn and drainage.

is famous for its asparagus. The salt marshes of Lincolnshire are home to succulent samphire.

Numerous windmills (a few still working) are reminders of the importance of grain in this area: there are hundreds of fields growing wheat, barley and oil-seed rape. The cultivation of sugar beet is important to the local economy and yellow fields of mustard have grown here ever since Jeremiah Colman started making his condiment near Norwich in 1814.

Soft fruits and orchards flourish in the region too, particularly around Wisbech in Cambridgeshire, and roadside stalls and pick-your-own farms are plentiful. Essex is a centre for jam-making, both cottage and commercial, and much of the produce is directed here. Then there are fruit juices and, in Lincolnshire, raspberry vinegar.

Above Rape seed is a modern crop that has quickly become an established part of the scenic landscape of Suffolk.

The seaside

Fishing has always been an important industry here, with large ports including Grimsby and Lowestoft handling a range of fish – cod, haddock, plaice, skate, sprats and turbot. In Southend there is an annual festival celebrating whitebait, small quantities of which are still landed there.

Great Yarmouth was once the centre for a huge herring fleet. The port bustled with workers dealing with up to 800,000 fish a day and there were large smokehouses at the docks sending smoked herrings, bloaters and kippers all over the world. As with many coastal towns, ecological influences and over-fishing have resulted in a major industry dwindling to almost nothing.

Shellfish thrive here, especially in the relatively shallow waters of the Wash. Cromer crabs, small but fleshy, can be bought at the roadside fresh or ready-dressed. There are cockles from Stiffkey and Leigh-on-Sea and whelks from Wells-next-the-Sea. Mussel beds are to

Maldon salt

The dry conditions on the Essex coast favour the production of sea salt, and the salt pans of Maldon are mentioned in the Domesday Book. The world-renowned Maldon crystal salt is soft and flaky, with a taste of the sea.

be found along the coasts of Norfolk and Lincolnshire. The native oysters from the beds at Colchester (England's first recorded town) are world famous, and the fishery here dates back to the Roman occupation. Farther north, at Brancaster, Pacific oysters are farmed.

In the Norfolk Broads the eel industry was once big and eels remain a local delicacy. Nowadays the waters are better known for pike and zander.

Pigs and turkeys

Though cattle and sheep are reared in East Anglia, pigs and poultry have always been preferred. In Essex the Dunmow Flitch trials are still held every

Below Kippers are still smoked in the traditional way in East Anglia.

three years, at which a flitch (side) of bacon is presented to a married couple who can prove they have not quarrelled in the previous year. Fidget (fitchet) pies with bacon, onions and apples are popular. Lincolnshire pork sausages and haslet are flavoured with sage. Stuffed chine – salt pork, slashed and filled with herbs – is a favourite.

Norfolk has been famed for its turkeys since flocks of traditional Norfolk Blacks were driven on the three-month journey to London in time for the Christmas market. Now it is home to a huge turkey farm. Historically, chickens, ducks, geese and guinea fowl have been reared in the region and conditions are ideal for game birds such as pheasant, partridge, woodcock and duck. All kinds of meat and fish are cured in the smokehouses of the Norfolk village of Orford.

Bread, cakes and puddings

The people of Cambridgeshire are said to have been the first to use a pudding cloth for wrapping and cooking suet puddings. Lincolnshire is perhaps best known for its plum bread and Grantham has its own gingerbread – a crunchy, puffed-up biscuit (cookie).

Above The seaflats of Maldon in Essex have provided superb quality salt since the 12th century.

Apples feature as an ingredient, and there are cake recipes using saffron, which serve as a reminder that the purple saffron crocus was once grown around Saffron Walden in Essex. In Norfolk, dumplings cooked on top of a stew are often called "swimmers".

Beer and wine

The region boasts several independent breweries making beer by traditional methods. Norfolk cider is usually made with cooking or dessert apples rather than the cider apples used in the West Country, so is less astringent. The climate suits grape growing, and vineyards in Essex, Norfolk and Suffolk produce a range of interesting wines.

The North-east

Above *The windswept and rugged landscape of the Yorkshire Dales.*

This region is notable for its beautiful, craggy coastline, reaching up to the border of Scotland and dotted with castles facing the North Sea. The heather-covered, rocky mountains of the Pennines lie to the west and there are dales and moors, seaside resorts and quaint fishing villages. Traditional meals tend to be simple, cheap, tasty and, in the cold climate of the North, warming. Little is wasted.

Fish, chips and kippers

The North Sea has been a great source of sustenance for the people of this region, providing a selection of fish and shellfish including cockles, mussels, scallops, crabs and lobsters. Whitby was once a great whaling port. The Yorkshire coble, a traditional "off the beach" fishing boat designed to be launched from steep shingle, is still used to work the inshore waters. The strong fishing heritage has resulted in a love of

fish and chips. This is the area to taste fish coated in a light, crisp batter, cooked in beef dripping, served with mushy peas and, of course, chips.

Northumberland has had a flourishing kipper industry based at Craster since the 19th century. It is still in business today, and herrings are split and hung from the rafters of the smokehouses before being smoked slowly and gently over the traditional fuel of smouldering oak chips.

Livestock and game

Plenty of high-quality beef is produced here – ideal for one of England's best-known meals: Roast Beef and Yorkshire Pudding. Yorkshire's famous batter pudding was originally cooked beneath the meat so that it caught and soaked up the juices and fat. It was made as one large pudding and would often be eaten as a first course, with gravy, before the roast: an idea developed in

> **Dock pudding**
> A springtime speciality enjoyed in West Yorkshire's Calder Valley is a pudding made with oatmeal, onions, nettles and "dock", or bistort, a species of knotweed. Once boiled the pudding is thickly sliced and fried in bacon fat.

lean days to reduce the diners' appetite for meat. In pubs and restaurants today, Yorkshire puddings are filled with sausages and gravy, mince or stew.

Sheep are the principal livestock of the region and the Yorkshire Moors and Yorkshire Dales are still home to some hardy breeds. Mutton was traditionally used in sausages, stews and pies, and

Below *This view of Lowther Castle, overlooking the snow-covered North Pennines, shows the grandeur of the highest parts of the region.*

Above *The pheasant became extinct in 17th-century England, but was successfully reintroduced in the 1830s.*

sheep's milk is made into interesting, distinctively flavoured local cheeses (including Yorkshire Blue).

As elsewhere, pigs have always played an important role too, with lard going to make cakes and pork pies. The famous York ham, traditionally eaten at Christmas, is prepared using the meat of the Large White pig, dry salted, smoked and hung.

The moors are ideal habitat for game, with fine grouse, partridge, pheasant, hare and deer to be had. Local dishes include jugged hare, game pies, patés and sausages.

Prize-winning vegetables and fruit

While most of the land is best suited to grazing, some is arable. Leeks grow especially well in this area and there are local competitions to discover the largest. Traditionally, leeks might be cooked in a pudding with suet pastry and served alongside meat stew. Pulses are popular and dishes containing peas were eaten regularly during Lent when meat was forbidden. In the 1800s, pease pudding was sold as street food.

Rhubarb growing is traditional in Yorkshire, notably in the "Rhubarb Triangle" between Pontefract, Wakefield and Leeds, which supplies the country with some of the finest forced rhubarb in early spring. Gooseberry showing is a tradition at the annual show in Egton Bridge, North Yorkshire. Growers return year after year to display traditional varieties and take part in a competition for the heaviest fruit. Bilberries (blueberries) grow wild on the moors and can be picked in late summer.

Below *The city of Newcastle has been enjoying a cultural renaissance and is now famous for its fine restaurants.*

The teashop

Baking is a strong northern tradition and the region's teashops serve buttered teacakes, rich fruitcakes, cakes and biscuits (cookies). Many puddings are enjoyed, including Yorkshire curd tart. Parkin, made with oatmeal and treacle (molasses), is traditionally eaten on Guy Fawkes Night on 5 November.

Bakestone cooking was popular here for oatcakes, drop scones, singin' hinnies and crumpets. Stottie cake, a savoury bread made with self-raising flour and milk, is traditional for bacon or chip butties. Traditional sweets include Harrogate toffee and Pontefract cakes, made from liquorice, which was once grown in the area.

Beer and holy brew

The region has a strong tradition of family-owned, independent breweries making strong beer. In pubs customers can be heard asking for "Newkie" or "brown dog" – Newcastle's famous brown ale. On Lindisfarne, just off the Northumberland coast, the monks of the 7th century brewed mead, which is still made there today.

Dales cheeses

Crumbly white Wensleydale cheese, made in Hawes in North Yorkshire, is traditionally eaten with rich fruitcake or Christmas cake. Cheese was made here in the Middle Ages by Cistercian monks, who brought cheese-making skills from Roquefort in France. Wensleydale almost went out of production in the 1990s, but as the favourite cheese of Wallace and Gromit it is now enjoying renewed success. Cotherstone, made in Teesdale, is a tangy, yellow cheese.

The North-west

This is a region of beautiful lakes, mountains and a dramatic coastline. It is protected by the Pennine range in the east and the Cheviots to the north. Between the hills and the Irish Sea lies the stunning area of the Lake District, together with manufacturing towns and plenty of farming land. Northern dishes were devised with hard-working people and big appetites in mind. They tend to be hearty and are often based on economical ingredients.

Meat, puddings and pies

The climate of the North-west of England is milder and wetter than that of the North-east and most of the land is given to grazing. Hardy breeds of sheep, chosen to withstand the cold and wind of the uplands, dot the hills and moorlands. Butchers' shops sell choice local lamb, which goes into

Below *The famous Swaledale sheep, with their distinctive black faces, roam free over the hills of the Lake District.*

classic local dishes such as Lancashire Hotpot and Shepherd's Pie. Mutton, which was once a staple throughout the country, is seeing a revival and is now reared in Cumbria. Wild game, including the succulent Derwentwater duck, also thrives on the uncultivated moors and mountains.

There is plenty of pork and bacon. Cumberland hams are dry cured, salted and rubbed with brown sugar. Meaty Cumberland sausage, seasoned with herbs and spices, is sold in a coil and bought by the length rather than by weight. Meats and sausages are often served with Cumberland sauce, made with redcurrant jelly, port, orange and spices. There is offal to be found that is now seldom seen in southern England: tripe and onions, brains, chitterlings (pig's intestines), elder (pressed cow's udder), lamb's fry (testicles) and sweetbreads. Pig's trotters and cow heel are used to enrich stews and to make jellied stock for pies. The North-west is black pudding (black sausage) country. The sausage-shaped puddings, made

from pig's blood and oatmeal, vary in texture and taste according to their maker. Secret recipes abound and there are competitions to discover the best. Faggots, potted meats, pressed tongue and brisket of beef are popular too.

Hot pies, both savoury and sweet, can be bought from stalls (especially popular at football matches), butchers, and fish and chip shops.

The dairy

The lush pastures of this region mean there is plenty of milk to make fine cream, butter and cheese. Dairy breeds such as Friesian are chosen for their high milk yields and are left to graze on the lowlands. Lancashire cheese has been made since the early 1900s and has a soft, crumbly texture and buttery flavour. Goats and sheep are kept for their milk too – for yogurt and cheeses.

In Cumberland, rum butter is a speciality that was traditionally served with oatcakes to visitors who had come to celebrate the birth of a baby.

Above *Herds of Freisian cows are a familiar sight in the North-west.*

Bays and lakes

Fishing has always been important to the region, with the industry centred in Fleetwood. Flatfish (such as plaice and sole), hake and herring (often stuffed and served with mustard sauce) are particularly popular. Morecambe Bay is famous for its small brown shrimps, which are potted in butter and sent all over the world.

Freshwater fish include trout and salmon in the lakes and rivers. It was traditional to catch them in the estuaries in wide "heave" or "haaf" nets, held by the fishermen standing in the water. Char is a fish special to the Lake District and is potted or used in pies. Found in the deep waters of the lakes, it is caught with long fishing lines. The Isle of Man is famed for kippers and tiny scallops.

Hardy crops

Lancashire is one of the few areas sheltered enough to grow vegetables. Varieties are chosen to suit the harsh climate, especially potatoes, root

vegetables and some salad plants. Little fruit is grown in the cold climate of this region, but damsons (known as witherslacks and grown around Lake Windermere) and gooseberries are notable exceptions.

Baked goods

This region offers a host of special cakes and pastries, such as Eccles cakes – flaky pastry cases stuffed full of currants, sugar and spices – and the Cumberland rum nicky, a pie with a similar filling doused in rum (rum was shipped here from the West Indies in the 1700s). Corners are large round pies cut into serving-size quarters.

Chester buns are made with yeast dough glazed with sugar and water. Chester cake is made with stale cake, treacle, currants and ginger, and cut into small squares after baking. Gingerbread has been made in Grasmere since the mid-19th century and the gingerbread shop is still there. Westmoreland pepper cake is a fruitcake spiced up with pepper. Goosnargh cakes from Lancashire, biscuit-like and flavoured with caraway seeds or coriander, were traditionally sold at Easter and Whitsun and served with a jug of ale. There are also curd tarts similar to those made in Yorkshire.

Above *Gooseberries are one of the few fruits grown in the North-west.*

Manchester tart has a shortcrust or puff pastry base spread with jam, topped with a layer of set custard and sprinkled with desiccated coconut.

Dense, chewy treacle toffee is popular here, while Everton toffee is crisp and flavoured with lemon. Kendal mint cake, the strongly peppermint-flavoured sweet, is taken on climbs and treks as a source of instant energy.

Below *The Old Dee Bridge, crossing the Dee at Chester, was built in 1387.*

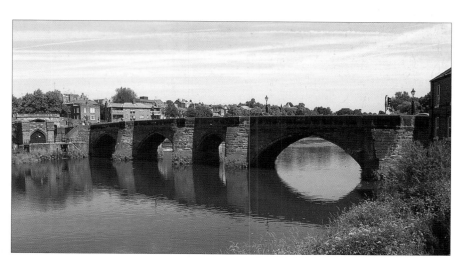

Feasts and festivals

Many of the annual feast days and festivals of England are linked to the Christian calendar, but their origins often stretch back to pre-Christian times, when pagan celebrations were inextricably linked with agriculture and seasonal change.

Shrove Tuesday

The last day before Lent, a period of fasting and reflection before the Christian celebration of Easter, is now often called Pancake Day. Shrove Tuesday is meant to be a day when everyone "shrives" or confesses their sins and receives absolution. It is also the last chance to feast before the period of abstinence. Pancakes are the customary treat, made with a batter containing the eggs, butter and milk that would otherwise go off during the 40 days of Lent. The traditions of tossing pancakes and pancake races are still kept up.

Good Friday

The day when Jesus Christ was crucified is a day of mourning in the Christian calendar, when churches are stripped of

Below A group of wartime evacuees celebrate Shrove Tuesday, by tossing pancakes into the air.

all decoration. It is traditional to eat fish on Good Friday, and hot cross buns are eaten warm for breakfast. Though the buns predated Christianity, they were adopted as a symbol of the cross on which Christ died.

In Tudor times spiced buns could, by law, be sold only on special days. Years ago hot cross buns were thought to have holy powers, and a bun would be hung from the ceiling to protect people in the house from harm. Bits of the stale bun would be grated off and used as a cure for illness, and if the bun went mouldy bad luck was to be had by all. There is a pub in London (The Widow's Son) where, in the early 19th century, a widow lived who was expecting her sailor son back home for Easter. On Good Friday she put a hot cross bun ready for him. Though the son never returned, his mother left the bun waiting and added a new one each year. When the house became a pub, the landlords continued the tradition.

Easter Day

Christians celebrate the resurrection of Jesus Christ on Easter Sunday, but many of the festival's symbols and traditions predate Christianity. Traditional foods include lamb (with rosemary for remembrance), simnel cake (a fruitcake layered with marzipan) and eggs (which

Above Families buy hot cross buns from a baker on a London street.

are forbidden during Lent). Customs include decorating eggs and egg hunts. In the north of England there is "egg jarping", when children tap their opponents' hard-boiled eggs with their own and the last to break is the champion, and "pace-egging", when they dress up and blacken their faces to go knocking on doors, asking in rhyme for Easter eggs. Egg rolling is still practised in England, when hard-boiled eggs are rolled down a hill. The winner might be the one that rolls the farthest or the one that survives best. Today chocolate eggs are given as gifts.

St George's Day

The patron saint of England, St George, is acknowledged on 23 April. Though there are no national celebrations people sometimes wear a red rose (the national flower), and some regions organize parades and concerts, while pubs and restaurants offer traditional English dishes.

Mothering Sunday

Also called Mother's Day, this was originally the day when people visited the "mother" church. In the 17th

century it became the occasion to acknowledge mothers. Children, mainly daughters, who had gone away to work as domestic servants were given a day off to visit their mother with flowers and simnel cake. Today it is a day when children give flowers, gifts and homemade cards to their mothers, and the family gathers for a meal.

May Day

The first day of May is the time to celebrate spring and the coming of summer. It once marked the time when livestock was moved to the hills to graze after a winter in the lowlands. It was customary to dance around the maypole (a surviving pagan symbol of virility from the festival of Beltane) and a May queen would be crowned with hawthorn blossoms. Houses were decorated with flowers, and young girls washed their faces in morning dew for a beautiful complexion. There might be processions and Morris dancing.

Halloween

The night of 31 October is All Hallows Eve, or Halloween. It is traditionally a night of witches, goblins, ghouls and

ghosts, a time of mischief, magic and mystery, with customs that can be traced back to the Celts. Fires would be lit on the hillsides to ward off evil spirits, and families huddled together at home out of harm's way. These days parties are held where lanterns with menacing faces are carved from pumpkins and swedes, and games such

Below A May day procession in a 19th century village with roots that go back to Beltane, the pagan spring festival.

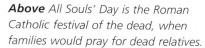

***Above** All Souls' Day is the Roman Catholic festival of the dead, when families would pray for dead relatives.*

as apple bobbing, when participants must remove apples from a bowl of water using only their teeth, are played.

All Souls' Day

Also with Celtic origins, All Souls' Day on 2 November was traditionally a solemn day of fasting, when Christians offered prayers for the dead. Flowers were put on graves, and candles and bonfires were lit to light the souls' way to the afterlife. It was the custom for the poor to offer prayers in return for money or food – especially fruit buns, which were called soul cakes. Spiced ale was served to the "soulers" and there were souling songs and plays.

Bonfire Night

The anniversary of the gunpowder plot on 5 November 1605 – when Guy Fawkes attempted (but failed) to blow up the Houses of Parliament in London with barrels of gunpowder – is still celebrated in England with bonfires and

Above *Traditional bonfire night food includes baked potatoes, sausages, treacle toffee and gingerbread.*

fireworks. It is traditional to burn an effigy, made by children from old clothes, paper and straw, to represent Guy Fawkes, and children would take their effigies onto the street asking for "a penny for the guy" with which to buy fireworks. In recent years the celebrations have developed into large organized events with spectacular firework displays.

Christmas

As Christians honour the birth of Jesus Christ at Christmas, families and friends come together to share customs and traditions that are centuries old. On Christmas Eve midnight mass is celebrated in churches all over the country, and children hang up stockings to be filled with gifts by Father Christmas, (provided they have been well-behaved all year).

On Christmas Day there is much feasting and good cheer. The boar's head was the centrepiece of the medieval feast, before goose, beef, chicken, and today's turkey replaced it.

Above *Wassailers in the 16th century, carrying a bowl of spiced ale to their neighbours in seasonal greeting.*

A Yule log was burned in every home, and is now represented by a cake. Plum pudding (made with prunes, eggs and meat) was the forerunner to Christmas pudding, with its rich mixture of dried fruit and spices. Similarly, mince pies were originally filled with a mixture of meat, dried fruit and spices, the meat survives in the form of suet in today's recipe. Mince pies were meant to bring good luck to those who ate one on each of the twelve days of Christmas.

Wassailing was once practised all over England. "Waes hael" was an Anglo-Saxon toast meaning "Good health", and a large bowl (the wassail bowl), filled with ale, spices and honey, would be passed round. It would be taken from door to door, and gifts of Christmas fare, drink or money were offered in exchange for a goodwill toast. Greetings cards, crackers and decorated trees became fashionable in Victorian times.

Below *The flaming Christmas pudding is carried in as the finale to the traditional Christmas Day dinner.*

Teatime traditions

Whether teatime is a quick cuppa and a biscuit at 4pm, a children's tea with sandwiches and cake, or a proper afternoon meal, the idea of teatime is embedded in the English psyche. Teatime might have had several changes since the 1600s, when leaf tea first arrived in England, but is still a familiar and well-loved ritual.

High tea

In the 19th century, as the working classes flocked to the cities to work in factories, the working day lengthened and the main meal of the day was served when they returned home in the evening at around 7pm. Breakfast was a modest affair, followed by a portable meal at midday. The evening meal often consisted of stews or meat puddings made with suet pastry – dishes that could be left all day to cook. Alternatively, it might be something that could be prepared quickly at the end of the working day, such as chops, kippers or perhaps cold meats, cheeses and pickles. Apple tart or milk pudding

Below *Afternoon tea, with the vicar, in an Edwardian garden: a quintessentially English scene.*

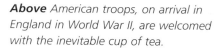

would follow and it would all be washed down with tea, which was by now England's most popular drink. It came to be known as high tea because it was eaten sitting "up" at the table, unlike afternoon tea.

Afternoon tea

The English ritual of afternoon tea is said to have begun in the 1840s, when the fashionable hour for dinner, the main meal of the day, had moved to around 8pm instead of 3 or 4 in the afternoon. A light meal at this time helped to ward off hunger pangs.

Above *American troops, on arrival in England in World War II, are welcomed with the inevitable cup of tea.*

When afternoon tea was introduced, it became an elegant social event with specific etiquette and smart dress, and was an ideal opportunity to show off fine china and silver. The meal was a light and leisurely affair that was conducted in the drawing room, front parlour or sitting room. China or Indian tea would be offered, together with a selection of sandwiches and cakes, the latter often made with fruit. At first the gatherings were made up mainly of middle- and upper- class ladies, and provided an opportunity to gossip. In the latter half of the 19th century, when hotels installed tearooms, and teashops opened, men began to join in.

Afternoon tea at home continued as a social occasion throughout the Edwardian period. Later, teatime gave women the chance to display their baking skills, but by the latter years of the 20th century, as more and more women took jobs outside the home, the ritual more or less disappeared. However, hotels and teashops continued to serve afternoon tea, and today it is possible to enjoy it in one form or another in towns and villages anywhere England.

Alcoholic beverages

With a beer industry dating back to the earliest times, cider drinking in the south-west, dark stouts in the north-east, wine imported from Europe long before the Romans came, and a long history of whisky appreciation, it is not surprising that many of England's favourite drinks are alcoholic. Much of the consumption of alcohol traditionally happens in public houses, or "pubs", which evolved from the taverns and coaching inns of the past. In their various manifestations, from Georgian drinking dens, to the men-only smoking clubs of the 1900s, to the smartened up gastro-pubs of today, pubs have held a central place in the social life of English adults.

Mead

In its simplest form, mead is a mixture of honey and water fermented with wild yeasts, and it is thought to be the oldest alcoholic drink in the world. The term "honeymoon" is thought to have originated in Anglo-Saxon times, when, for a month after the wedding, the bride's father would supply his son-in-law with all the mead he could drink in the belief that it aided fertility.

The art of making mead had been preserved for centuries in monasteries, until their dissolution during the reign of Henry VIII. By the 17th century, imports of cheap sugar from the West Indies had reduced the importance of honey as a sweetener and it was no longer essential for everyone to keep bees. Mead-making declined and never really recovered, but the drink can still be found, made by artisan producers all over the country.

Beer and ale

Ale is simply fermented grain and has been drunk throughout England's history as a healthy alternative to water, which was often contaminated. Taverns existed as far back as Roman times but it was the Normans who first organized brewing on a larger scale, setting up breweries attached to abbeys and monasteries for the refreshment of monks and travellers. By the Middle Ages, the brewing of ale was largely the realm of women; alehouses were well established and ale was the most common drink, even for children. There were strong ales, medicinal varieties and weak versions for children.

Until the 15th century ale consisted of malted barley, water and yeast. Then merchants from Flanders and Holland introduced a new brewing method to England. The new hopped version was called beer. It had a bitter flavour and, unlike ale, kept well. By the 18th century all beers were hopped.

Most brewing took place in the home until the increase in commercial brewing in the 19th century. Various styles of beer have developed, with each differing according to the water

Below *Coaching inns, set every seven miles along England's roads, stabled horses, and fed travellers, throughout the 18th and 19th centuries. Many still survive as roadside pubs today.*

Above The interior of a traditional public house in the 1800s.

Above A country pub today, virtually unchanged in over 200 years.

supply – pale beer, dark beer, porter and stout. The 21st century has seen a significant revival in specialist brews.

Cider

Pressing and fermenting apples to make cider is an ancient art. New apple varieties reached England with the Romans and later with the Normans. By

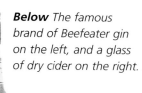

Below The famous brand of Beefeater gin on the left, and a glass of dry cider on the right.

the middle of the 17th century, cider-making had reached a peak and most farms had a cider orchard and an apple press. The drink was popular with all and it became traditional to pay part of a farm labourer's wages in cider, with extra at haymaking time, though consumption declined as farming practices changed. As the population moved from the farms to the towns in the 19th century, commercial cider-making developed. Today, small-scale and artisan producers coexist happily with the large manufacturers.

Gin

Cheap gin had a huge impact on English society in the 1700s, when its abuse by the poor became a major problem. When it was first introduced from the Netherlands, gin was drunk for medicinal purposes, but because it was very cheap it soon became a drink of the poor. By the mid-18th century London alone had more than 7,000 gin shops and 11 million gallons of gin were distilled there every year. Workers were given gin as part of their wages and much of it was drunk by women. The Gin Acts of 1729 and 1736

attempted to curb consumption by making the drink prohibitively expensive, but could not be enforced; riots ensued and distilling (and consumption) continued. In the 1750s new licensing and excise policies were introduced, and slowly the problem was resolved. In the 19th century, beer shops and public houses became popular and the interest in gin waned.

Below A pint of traditionally brewed real ale, as popular as ever in England.

Cheese-making

In England cheese has a long history, and there was a time when it was made in almost every farmhouse. During spring and summer there was plenty of milk available (from ewes, goats and cows), and making it into cheese meant that it could be kept without spoiling to feed the family during the winter months. Cheese-making was a skill that was passed down through generations of families and farmers.

Ancient cheeses

For the Romans, cheese was an everyday food and soldiers were given a small ration every day. They are thought to have taken England's oldest cheese, Cheshire, back to Rome with them. In the 11th century the Normans brought their cheese-making expertise to England, and much of it was made by monks. With the dissolution of the monasteries, the business of making cheese passed to the farmers' wives.

The upper classes enjoyed rich, creamy cheeses, leaving very hard

Above *Local cheeses, such as Cheddar and Wensleydale, are often named after the places they are produced in.*

cheeses made from skimmed milk for the poor. In the Middle Ages cheese made from surplus milk would be sold at cheese fairs and local markets, a tradition that continues today. By the

17th century, every region was producing its own distinctive cheese, with characteristics depending on the breed of animal, pasture and individual recipes or preferences.

Industrialization

Commercial cheese-making began in England during the Industrial Revolution, when workers migrated from the country to the towns. To supply this new and growing market, creameries were set up with factories making cheese on a large scale from the milk of mixed cattle herds from a wide area. With farmers selling their milk direct to the manufacturers, the production of local cheeses began to go into decline.

During World War II farmhouse cheese-making was again severely reduced and what little cheese was made was mass produced in factories. When rationing ended – and a greater choice of cheese became available – it became fashionable in some circles for a while to host cheese and wine parties.

Below *Acidity levels of cheese are carefully checked in a large cheese dairy near Reading, in Berkshire.*

Artisanal cheeses

While cheeses continue to be manufactured on a large scale, recent years have seen a revolution in the English cheese industry. In spite of commercial pressures and government regulations, a new generation is discovering the art of cheese-making. With skill and passion it is reviving traditional recipes, and developing new ones using old techniques, to produce an enormous range of handcrafted cheeses with styles and flavours that are varied and unique. Milk is being sourced from rare breeds, and regions that do not have a long tradition of cheese-making are creating exciting new products.

An increasing number of cheeses are now being granted PDO (Protected Designation of Origin), an endorsement intended to protect the name, heritage and tradition of regional foods from imitation by mass producers. Stilton, West Country Farmhouse Cheddar and Single Gloucester are all examples of PDO cheeses.

An important part of the resurgence of locally produced, specialist cheeses is the growing number of dedicated cheese shops that sell a wide variety:

cheeses made with the milk of cows, goats, ewes and even buffaloes; hard-pressed and soft cheeses; cheeses wrapped in cloth, rolled in herbs or wrapped in leaves; and cheeses washed in cider, perry, brandy or brine. There are food trails featuring cheese, cheese festivals and annual cheese awards. The cheeseboards of more and more pubs and restaurants feature good local and regional English cheeses.

Below Young cheese maturing on racks at Sharpham House Dairy in Devon.

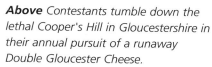

Above Contestants tumble down the lethal Cooper's Hill in Gloucestershire in their annual pursuit of a runaway Double Gloucester Cheese.

Making farmhouse cheese

The milk from the morning or evening milking (or a mixture of the two) may be left whole, skimmed, semi-skimmed or enriched with cream. The prepared milk is warmed and soured (or acidified) by adding a starter culture – a blend of bacteria that occur naturally in milk. When the correct acidity has been reached, rennet (or a vegetarian equivalent) is added, causing the milk to coagulate and separate into solid curds and liquid whey. The curd is cut to break it up (lightly for soft cheese and finely for hard cheese) and the whey is drained off. The curds are shaped or tipped into moulds, and left to finish draining or pressed to remove moisture. The more the curd is pressed, the firmer the cheese will be.

Many English cheeses are "ripened" or matured for some time (up to 18 months), during which a mould develops on the surface, or the cheese develops a rind. Alternatively, they may be coated in leaves or wax.

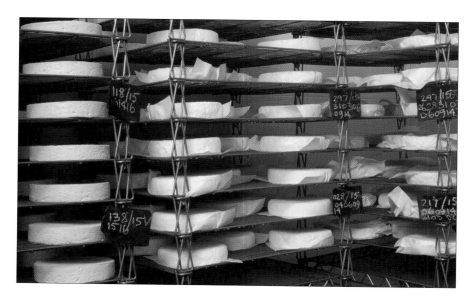

Bread-making

Before the Romans arrived, cereal grains such as barley and wheat were crushed by hand, made into rough bread and cooked over open fires. With the Romans came the harnessing of water and animals to mill grain. They greatly increased the cultivation of wheat, which was even exported to feed their armies in Europe. The Roman bread oven, similar to today's wood-fired pizza oven, replaced open-fire baking.

Loaves for rich and poor

The departure of the Romans saw a decline in the use of wheat and the arrival of rye with the Saxons and Danes. Rye was ideal for growing in the northerly climate, and the resulting dark bread became a staple food. In the Middle Ages, the invention of hair sieves meant the bran could be sifted from wheat flour to make finer, whiter bread. Bread became an indication of status, with the rich eating

Below Before the Romans introduced the enclosed oven to England, bread was always cooked on an open fire.

small white wheaten loaves called manchets while the poor ate the coarse dark bread made from barley, rye or mixed grains. The most common bread, "maslin", was made from a mixture of rye and wheat. The bread of the poor usually contained weed seeds and when grain was in short supply, ground beans, peas and even acorns were added to bulk it out.

By the 11th century watermills had become the main method of milling and the building of watermills at large ports encouraged the importation of grain. In the 12th century windmills began to spring up, allowing grain to be milled in locations where there was no fast-flowing water.

The rise of the loaf

In Georgian times, thanks to improvements in agriculture, wheat began to overtake rye and barley to become the most popular grain for bread-making. The introduction of sieves made of Chinese silk helped to produce even finer and whiter flour, though bakers were often accused of

Above Factory-produced bread became widespread during World War II, when the National Loaf was introduced.

adulterating bread by using alum, lime, chalk and powdered bones to keep it very white. Previously the preserve of the rich, white bread gradually became more generally available. Tin from the flourishing mines in Cornwall began to be used to make baking tins. This produced rectangular loaves that could be sliced and toasted – and it was not long before the sandwich was invented.

The Corn Laws of the early 19th century, which prohibited the importation of grain to protect the interests of landowners, kept bread prices high and starvation became a serious threat to the poor, particularly after the failure of the Irish potato crop. Eventually the Corn Laws were repealed and the duty on imported grain was removed. The subsequent influx of good-quality North American wheat enabled white bread to be made at a reasonable cost. Steel roller mills gradually replaced watermills and windmills, and in 1930 the pre-packed sliced loaf appeared in Britain, to an enthusiastic welcome.

Above The bloomer is one of England's traditionally shaped loaves.

The health benefits of wholemeal flour and bread had been identified in the early 20th century, but this failed to change the nation's overwhelming preference for white bread. However, during World War II, the "National Loaf", roughly equivalent to today's brown bread, was introduced due to a shortage of shipping space for white flour. Calcium was added to the flour to prevent rickets, which was found to be common in women joining the Land Army, and when the National Loaf was abolished, new laws dictated that all flour other than wholemeal had to be fortified with calcium, iron, Vitamin B1 (thiamin) and nicotinic acid.

Industrial bread production

As bread production and distribution became more efficient, and the first supermarkets appeared, the country saw a decline in small master bakers and the emergence of large companies. In 1965 the Chorleywood Bread Process was adopted. By a combination of chemical additives and high-speed

mixing this substantially reduced the period of fermentation, reducing the time taken to produce a loaf and at the same time using an increased proportion of homegrown wheat. The result was standardized, inexpensive loaves. The demand for sliced, wrapped bread grew until, at the end of the 20th century, a loaf of bread cost very little.

Today, while the wrapped, sliced loaf remains popular, there is a strong demand for bread prepared and baked

Above Stoneground flour has seen a revival in popularity in recent years.

by traditional methods. There is a welcome revival of traditional milling and the return of master bakers offering breads made with a variety of different flours and grains.

Below Small bakers, using traditional bread-making methods, are a welcome alternative to mass-produced bread.

The English Kitchen

The range of ingredients produced in England is varied –
from its fields, orchards and hedgerows to its hillsides and
lowland pastures; and from its rivers and lakes to
extensive coastlines. The seasonal and regional qualities of
these ingredients continue to boost England's growing
reputation for good food, and their diversity and
provenance encourage the cook to prepare delicious
dishes, both traditional and modern.

Vegetables

Since the Romans brought cultivated varieties to England, vegetables have played an important role in the English diet. In a short time the Celtic diet of wild plants and roots grew to include a range of grown and harvested vegetables. Fields of beans and peas were common by the Middle Ages, and explorers returned to Tudor England with potatoes and other exotics. Most vegetables were boiled and served with butter, but when the new landowners of the 17th century created kitchen gardens, cooking methods became more adventurous.

When transport improved, vegetables could be enjoyed outside their traditional growing areas, and by the late 20th century they were being imported from all over the world. Suddenly most vegetables were available all year round, often cheaper than those grown in England. Today there is revived interest in the growing and eating of local, seasonal produce, and more shops and farmers' markets are offering high-quality local produce, some of it organically grown.

Below Today's bright orange carrots have developed from an early variety that was purple in colour.

Beneath the soil

Carrot Every cook's standby for a side dish to accompany meat or fish, carrots are also used to give their flavour and sweetness to soups and casseroles. In the 18th and 19th centuries, they were much used in sweet puddings and tarts.

Parsnip is now a popular vegetable. Steam or boil it lightly, mash it (perhaps mixed with carrots or potatoes), roast it or add it to soups and stews.

Turnip The sweet, peppery flavour of the white turnip is best appreciated in spring and early summer, when it goes especially well with lamb and duck.

Swede Larger than turnip and with a leathery purple skin, swede (rutabaga) has a firm flesh and a sweet taste that is quite distinctive. It is usually eaten mashed with plenty of butter.

Potato When the potato was introduced to England in the late 16th century, it took a long time to become accepted. Today there are many varieties, and there is a potato to suit every cooking method and every meal.

Onions Introduced into England by the Romans, by the Middle Ages onions, together with cabbage and beans, were one of the three main vegetables eaten by rich and poor.

Above Parsnips were once only used for animal consumption.

Above The horseradish root was used as a medicine in the Middle Ages.

Horseradish When grated and mixed with cream it makes a sauce that is a perfect accompaniment to roast beef.

Jerusalem artichoke This knobbly tuber is a relative of the sunflower. Serve it roasted, boiled, mashed or in soup.

Beetroot (beet) Often cooked and pickled for salad, it can also be boiled or roasted and served hot.

Below Homegrown potatoes played a major role in feeding the population during the two World Wars.

Above Traditional village shows are still held in the north east of England to find the largest leek.

Above For a brief few weeks in spring, England produces some of the best asparagus in the world.

Above Globe artichokes were once thought to be an aphrodisiac, perhaps because of the way they are eaten.

Above the soil

Leek With its delicate onion flavour, the leek is good in many dishes, including soups, pies, sauces and stews.

Celery After the Romans brought celery to England, it grew wild and tough until the 18th century, when it was cultivated. Now we enjoy pale green summer celery and white winter celery.

Cauliflower This grows particularly well in the south-west of England and is traditionally served with cheese sauce.

Below Thought to have originated in the eastern Mediterranean, cauliflower was bought to England by the Romans.

Asparagus Once known by the name of sparrowgrass, asparagus was popular with the Romans and has been grown in English country gardens ever since the 16th century. East Anglia and the Vale of Evesham are the traditional growing areas.

Cabbage is one of the oldest vegetables and is easy to grow. The English enjoy several varieties – green, white and red – with the wrinkly Savoy and young spring greens being particularly popular. Available all year round, cabbage can be boiled, steamed or stir-fried.

Brussels sprouts look and taste like tiny cabbages. They are served as a side vegetable (traditionally mixed with chestnuts at Christmas) or thinly sliced and served raw or stir-fried.

Globe artichoke is an edible thistle, with layers of leaves surrounding the central heart. It is good boiled and served with lemon butter, for dipping the base of the leaves and the hearts.

Spinach When spinach arrived in England from Spain, where it was introduced by the Moors, it was referred to as "the Spanish vegetable". The small young leaves add a mildly peppery taste to salads.

Peas and beans have been around since the Middle Ages, when they were grown and dried to feed families through the winter.

Pumpkin adds its colour to autumn, when it is traditional to carve orange pumpkins into lanterns for Halloween and use the flesh to make soup. Other varieties of squash, can be mashed, fried, roasted or stuffed and baked.

Chard Similar to spinach, older chard has tough stems that need to be cooked longer than the leaves.

Below Unlike most vegetables, peas freeze well and are a staple vegetable standby in most English homes.

Fruits

England's temperate climate is ideal for growing orchard and soft fruits, and many regions still grow the same varieties that they have for centuries.

Orchard fruits

Traditional orchards have long been a distinctive feature of the English landscape, particularly in the heartlands of Kent, Gloucestershire and Herefordshire. However, recent years have seen a severe decline in orchard-fruit crops and many old English varieties have disappeared. Fortunately, traditional fruit growers are now beginning to see a turnaround, with some supermarkets responding to consumers' demand for home-grown produce, and local shops and farmers' markets helping to bring back traditional varieties.

Apples The ancestor of the modern apple is the crab apple, with its small sour fruits that make delicious jellies and other preserves. There is a huge range of traditional apple varieties, each with its own texture and unique flavour, and many are evocatively named. Dessert apples include Ashmead's Kernel, Blenheim Orange, Cox's Orange Pippin, Discovery, James Grieve, Knobby Russet, and Worcester Pearmain. Varieties that are more suitable for

Below *The apple is England's oldest and most loved fruit.*

Above *Most medieval English pears came from stock brought from France.*

cooking include Bramley's Seedling, Burr Knot, Golden Hornet, Norfolk Beauty and Smart's Prince Arthur. English cider apples include Bulmer's Norman, Hoary Morning and Slack-me-girdle. Apple traditions such as apple bobbing and toffee apples survive to this day.

Pears The pear's history can be traced back almost as far as the apple and for a long time it was considered the superior fruit. By the 19th century there were hundreds of varieties. Today the most popular English dessert pear is the Conference, long and thin with green skin tinged with russet, and sweet flesh. Williams pears (known as Bartlett in the USA and Australia), bred in Berkshire in the 18th century, are golden yellow or red-tinged and are ideal for cooking.

Plums Originally cultivated from hedgerow fruits – the cherry plum and the sloe – plums vary in colour from black to pale green and yellow and can be sweet or tart. In England they were grown in the gardens of medieval monasteries. The Victoria plum was first cultivated in Sussex in the 1800s and, with its red and yellow skin,

Above *The Victoria plum is popular cooked in pies, crumbles and puddings.*

remains the most popular dessert plum. The greengage is a sweet amber-coloured plum that makes particularly good jam. Damsons are small plums with dark blue-to-purple skins and yellow flesh. They give their colour and flavour to damson gin.

Cherries These are grouped into three main types: sweet, acid and sour (known as Dukes). Sweet cherries can

Below *Fruit pies, in particular apple, are a favourite dessert in England.*

be firm and dry, ideal for candying into glacé cherries, or soft and juicy. Acid cherries, of which the Morello is the best known, range in colour from pale to those with an intense crimson glow. Duke cherries are thought to be crosses between these two.

Quince The quince is an apple- or pear-shaped fruit with scented yellow flesh. Because it is very hard it needs long slow cooking. It is lovely cooked with apples or pears, when only a small amount is needed to add its flavour. Quinces make good jams and jellies that go well with pork.

Medlar Though rare today, these small brown fruits with their sharp flavour can still be found in the warmer areas of England. They are only edible raw and only when overripe.

Berries, currants and rhubarb

Local farmers' markets and pick-your-own farms are the best sources of traditional English varieties of soft fruit.

Strawberries are possibly England's most popular summer fruit. While Elsanta has become the most frequently grown variety, Cambridge Favourite, English Rose, Hapil and Royal Sovereign

Below Strawberries and cream are an important part of an English summer.

Above Once only available from autumn hedgerows, blackberries are now cultivated for sale year-round.

are becoming popular again. Strawberries are a traditional feature of the Wimbledon tennis championships.

Raspberries are soft, juicy, sweet yet acidic, and can be red, yellow, white and black. Fresh raspberries are enjoyed on their own, with cream, or can be added to desserts, sauces, ice creams, james and flavoured vinegars.

Blackberries English cooks often mix blackberries with apples in fruit pies and puddings, and they make lovely jam and jelly. The cultivated fruits are larger and juicier than the wild bramble, but many people pick wild blackberries from the hedgerows in early autumn. It is considered bad luck to gather them after Michaelmas Day (29 September): according to folklore, it is the day on which Satan was cast out of heaven and fell into a blackberry bush; in vengeance, on that day every year, he spits or stamps on the berries.

Mulberries look similar to, though larger than, blackberries, and can be used in the same ways. They are the fruit of large, long-lived trees of Asian origin, which have probably been grown in England since Roman times. Mulberries are very soft and easily damaged so are not widely available commercially, but are delicious straight from the tree.

Currants Blackcurrants, with their rich, slightly sour flavour, are the most commonly used. Red and white currants are delicious mixed with other summer fruits in a summer pudding.

Above Redcurrants make a jelly, often eaten with roast chicken or turkey.

Gooseberries belong to the currant family and have always been especially popular in England. They can be round, long, hairy or smooth, and different varieties are suitable for cooking or eating raw. They ripen when the elder tree is in flower, and elderflowers are traditionally added to impart a delicious muscatel flavour.

Rhubarb is botanically a vegetable, but it is used like a fruit. The tender pink stems of early forced rhubarb are a spring treat, mostly grown in Yorkshire. Main crop rhubarb, with its thick stems, stronger colour and more acidic flavour, is eaten in pies and crumbles.

Below Gooseberries come in to season in June, a welcome early summer fruit.

48

Fish

England has always enjoyed a wonderful variety of fish from its coastal waters, lakes and rivers. Recent years have seen fish stocks diminish, and the varieties of fish appreciated today are few compared to those eaten in the past, but an increase in fish farming has led to greater availability of certain species such as salmon and trout.

Cooking fish

Fresh fish benefits from simple methods of cooking, such as frying, grilling, steaming or baking. In restaurants fish is frequently served with classic (often French) sauces, but the vegetation from the natural habitat of the fish, and perhaps on which the fish feeds, often makes the best accompaniment; enhancing its natural flavour.

Freshwater fish from clean waters need only simple cooking and delicate herbs such as watercress or thyme, perhaps with melted butter, to bring out their natural flavours. Sea fish can take more robust flavours, such as samphire, sauces made from shellfish, and herbs with strong flavours. Oily fish such as herring and mackerel are often cooked coated in oatmeal, which absorbs their strong flavours. Some species are best cooked whole, while others are better filleted.

Sea fish

Several species have been affected by over-fishing and stocks are desperately low. Cod and haddock are two examples of species where reduced

Above Turbot is highly prized and can be cooked in a variety of ways.

Above Herring is often smoked, after which it is called a kipper.

numbers have led to higher prices. Nevertheless, both fish remain popular, and are sold as steaks, cutlets and fillets. Haddock, while smaller than cod, has a pronounced flavour that many

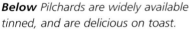

Below Pilchards are widely available tinned, and are delicious on toast.

people consider to be finer, and in the north-east of England it is always the first choice for fish and chips. Both haddock and cod are good baked, poached, grilled or fried (with or without batter). Other white fish, which vary in availability and popularity, include hake, with its firm flesh, pollack, whiting and coley, all of which are excellent in pies, soups and stews.

Plaice is a popular flat fish with a good flavour and texture. Available whole or as fillets, it is suitable for rolling and stuffing, grilling, frying, steaming and poaching. Dover sole has a firm texture and a fine

Above Cod stocks have suffered from over-fishing in English waters.

Above *Mackerel has always been plentiful in England's coastal waters.*

flavour that is best appreciated when the fish is simply grilled on the bone, perhaps with melted butter, chopped parsley and lemon juice. Lemon sole has softer flesh and a flavour not quite as fine as that of Dover sole, but it too is popular, being less expensive and suitable for serving with strongly flavoured sauces.

Turbot is considered by many to be the aristocrat of fish, with a sweet flavour and firm white flesh that can stand up to robust kinds of cooking. Halibut is widely available as fillets and steaks; it is best for grilling, frying or baking, but it can be poached or steamed, too.

Herrings, sprats, pilchards, sardines and whitebait are all members of the same family, with a similar texture and bold flavours. England's thriving herring industry ensured they were always cheap and they remain good value today. The larger fish are delicious fried, grilled (especially on the barbecue) or baked. Tiny whitebait are deep fried and eaten whole, and remain a popular appetizer in restaurants, particularly in London where they were once so

Right *Brown river trout has a lovely flavour, and is ideal grilled or baked.*

plentiful that they were sold from barrows in the streets. The pilchard has long been a mainstay of the Cornish fishing industry, though in greater demand abroad than at home: most of the fish has traditionally been salted and exported to France and Italy. The oil that drained from the fish during processing, known as "train oil", was once used for lighting as a cheaper alternative to candles. Nowadays, with smaller catches and higher prices, the fresh fish is being more alluringly re-marketed in England under the name "Cornish sardine".

Mackerel also remains inexpensive and is much enjoyed grilled or baked in the oven, or cooked on the barbecue.

Several other species are still caught around the English coast, albeit in smaller quantities, including brill, dabs, skate, sea bass, monkfish, ling, John Dory, gurnard and red mullet.

Below *Much of the salmon eaten in England is farmed, but wild fish is still available from good fishmongers.*

Freshwater fish

England's rivers used to team with a large variety of freshwater fish, and most large country estates would have had at least one pond stocked with perch, pike and other species.

Salmon is one of today's most popular fish – it certainly appears on almost every restaurant menu in the country – due to the dramatic increase in fish farming around Britain. Salmon is perfect for cooking whole and is a favourite centrepiece for summer entertaining. Fillets and steaks are lovely pan-fried, grilled or barbecued. Salmon caught "in the wild", as they return from the sea to the rivers where they

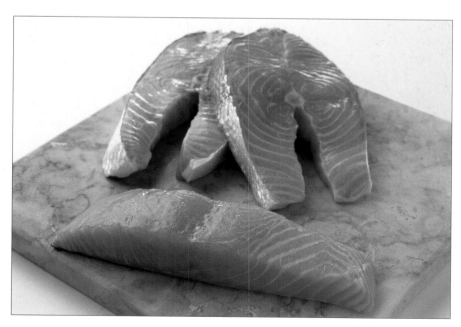

Above *Once cooked, crayfish become a much more appetizing pink colour.*

were born each summer to spawn, are a seasonal treat and worth the high prices they command. Salmon trout, otherwise known as sea trout or sewin, has become an endangered species. With its firm pink flesh and delicate flavour, it combines the best qualities of salmon and trout, and can be cooked in exactly the same way as salmon.

The native brown trout, which is biologically identical to the salmon trout but not migratory, is found in lakes and streams in several regions. Due to the success of fish farming, rainbow trout is now widely available and inexpensive.

Below *In 17th-century England, oysters were so plentiful they were fed to cats.*

Right *The little brown shrimps caught in Morecambe Bay are potted and exported around the world.*

Both kinds of trout can be enjoyed poached, baked, fried or grilled.

English rivers and lakes are also home to grayling, pike, zander, perch, roach, tench, bream, crayfish, eels and elvers.

Shellfish

In the past, some species of shellfish were so plentiful that they were considered food for the poor. The coastlines of the north-east and south-west in particular have been good sources of shellfish, including lobster, crab, scallops, clams and mussels. The English have always been partial to a bag of whelks, winkles or cockles, freshly cooked in a beach-side hut or bought from the street sellers in and around London.

These days, English oysters are celebrated as a delicacy, eaten raw, and are at their best from late autumn to spring – they are traditionally eaten only

Below *English mussels are still plentiful, inexpensive and easy to prepare.*

"when there is an R in the month". Whitstable in Kent and Lindisfarne in Northumberland are both renowned for oysters. Morecambe Bay on the north-west coast is famous for its tiny brown shrimps, and many sandy estuaries are home to razor clams. As with other fish, shellfish stocks have been in decline in recent years, and many sheltered bays and estuaries are now home to aquaculture farms growing mussels, oysters, clams and scallops.

Smoked fish

Before the days of refrigeration, freezing and easy transport, smoking over peat or wood fires was one of the chief methods of preserving fish. Smoked fish could be kept for times when fresh food was not so plentiful and for the many days when Christians were obliged to abstain from eating meat. Nowadays fish is smoked for the distinctive flavour it imparts rather than the need to preserve it. Fish that is smoked naturally is far superior to that with added dye and flavourings.

Some fish, such as salmon, trout, mackerel or herring, is hot smoked, which means it is gently cooked as it is smoked and is therefore ready for eating. Cold smoking involves smoking the fish very gently over a long period over a smouldering fire. Cold-smoked fish needs either to be cooked first, as in the case of kippers or smoked

Right *Kippers are mostly eaten at breakfast time in England.*

haddock, or cut into wafer-thin slices and served raw, sprinkled with lemon juice, like salmon, trout or mackerel.

Though Scotland is the main British producer of smoked fish, especially salmon, England has always had its share of smokehouses. The south-west, and Cornwall in particular, is known for its smoked mackerel, kippers and bloaters. On the east coast, Great Yarmouth once bustled with fish workers and smokehouses producing bloaters and kippers. In Northumberland smoked fish is also a

Below *Smoked haddock makes a delicious addition to fish pie.*

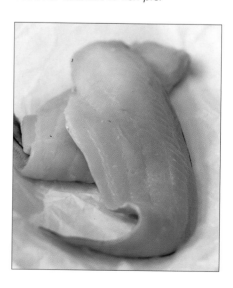

Above *Thin slices of smoked salmon are hugely popular as a starter.*

speciality, especially salmon and kippers. In fact, oak-smoked kippers were first made in the fishing town of Seahouses, and kippers are still produced in traditional smokehouses there and just down the coast at Craster.

Smoked herrings Bloaters are lightly smoked and dry-salted herrings that have had their heads, tails and bones removed. They are best grilled or fried. Buckling are whole, hot-smoked herring that are ready to eat. Kippers are herrings that have been split, slightly salted and cold smoked. They are poached or grilled. Red herrings are whole herrings that have been heavily smoked and salted and have a strong flavour. They are still obtainable from a few artisan smokers and can be eaten cold or lightly grilled.

Smoked haddock is traditionally served poached for breakfast or supper.

Smoked salmon is served in wafer-thin slices with lemon wedges for squeezing over, black pepper and brown bread.

Smoked trout can be bought whole or in fillets and is good as an appetizer or

made into spreads and patés. It can also be served with salad as a main course.

Smoked mackerel, with its rich flavour and smooth texture, is enjoyed in salads or made into spreads and patés.

Smoked eel is a delicacy that was formerly difficult to find, but now smokeries in East Anglia and Somerset are encouraging a revival by offering it in chunks, ready to eat.

Below *Smoked eel is a neglected delicacy that is enjoying a resurgence.*

Meat

The English have always enjoyed home-reared meat of excellent quality and good flavour. For the wealthy and middle classes it was the mainstay of their diet but the peasant class would only eat it on festivals and holidays.

Before the introduction of the modern oven, particularly in large houses, meat was cooked in huge joints, roasted on a spit in front of the kitchen fire. The less wealthy, meanwhile, would take their meat to be cooked in the baker's oven while they attended church on Sunday morning. It was customary to make the Sunday joint last for several days: it would be served hot or cold, and made into dishes such as pies, rissoles and bubble and squeak. While modern ovens are designed to cook smaller pieces of meat, the Sunday roast (especially roast beef) remains a traditional family and celebratory meal.

The traditional butcher, with sound knowledge and expertise, has always been the best source. A good supplier will know when it is appropriate to hang meat before selling, and for how

Below *The classic English Sunday dinner: a wonderful joint of roast beef.*

long, in order to achieve the best texture and flavour. In recent years there has been a serious decline in the number of independent butchers in England, but some excellent ones remain, supported by loyal customers. More and more farmers are selling direct from the farm or at farmers' markets.

Pork, bacon and ham

The pig has played a most important role in England's eating. There was a time when at least one pig was reared in every cottage, farm and country house in every village and town, fed on household scraps and often on the whey left over from cheese-making. The "porker" would be kept from springtime until autumn, when it was slaughtered. In small communities, pigs would be killed a few at a time and the meat shared out between neighbours. This practice continued until the late 19th century, when it was no longer permissible to keep pigs near the home.

When there was plenty of meat the people ate to "lay on fat" before winter set in. The boar was saved for Christmas and went into mince pies, with the head being reserved for the table centrepiece. In the new year, the long sides (flitches) of bacon cured in autumn saw the family through the lean months until spring. Most parts of the pig were cured to make bacon,

Above *There are several regional types of sausage, including Cumberland, which is sold coiled into a circle.*

Left *There are many different cuts of pork, and many ways of cooking it.*

though the offal would be eaten immediately and some fresh pork would be cooked too. The legs were reserved for ham. Every part of the animal was eaten, including trotters, stomach wall (tripe), brain, tongue, ears and tail; the blood was used for black pudding (blood sausage). Traditional breeds are seeing a revival today – such as the ginger-haired Tamworth and Gloucester Old Spot, often called the orchard pig because it was fattened on windfalls.

Below *Tripe is still eaten in England. Traditionally it is cooked with onions.*

Above *Black pudding is a much-loved breakfast food in the Midlands.*

As well as remaining the foundation of the English breakfast, bacon is used to flavour all kinds of dishes, including soups, stews and stuffings. Pork is enjoyed roasted, perhaps with a stuffing of sage and onion, and served with apple sauce. It is made into sausages, pork pies, black puddings, haslet and many other regional dishes.

Mutton and lamb

Lamb as we know it today was once unheard of. Sheep have always been raised more extensively than pigs or cattle and almost always grazed on grassland. Originally, sheep were kept

Below *A rack of lamb ribs makes a quick and delicious roast meal.*

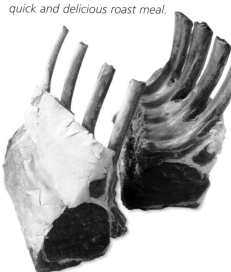

primarily for their wool. All sheep meat was mutton – with a strong flavour and texture that required slow cooking to tenderize it. Over the years, lamb has slowly replaced mutton: young, tender and sweet, it can be cooked quickly to suit modern lifestyles. Lamb joints are roasted and served with mint sauce or redcurrant jelly, while chops and steaks are grilled, fried or barbecued. Lamb is the basis of traditional dishes such as Lancashire Hotpot and Shepherd's Pie.

Today, there is spring lamb from southern England, followed by hill lamb from northern areas and lamb (up to 18 months old) from all over the country. Hogget (one to two years old) and mutton (over two years) are experiencing a welcome revival. Specialist breeds are available from farmers' markets and traditional butcher shops, with interesting names such as Blackface, Blue-faced Leicester, Lincoln Longwool, Norfolk Horn, Texel and White-faced Woodland. There is Romney from the salt marshes of Kent, and mutton in the shape of the Ryeland and Herdwick breeds.

Beef

Cattle are reared for both their milk and their meat. Old breeds still raised in England today include the Shorthorn (in the north) and the Red Poll (in eastern areas). The British White was always popular on the estates of large houses. Selective breeding means that there are now cattle suited to all kinds of terrain – lowlands, hills and moorlands – with breeds such as the Hereford, South Devon and Sussex providing meat that is marbled with fat and has an excellent flavour.

These days prime cuts of beef are an expensive luxury, but roast beef with all the trimmings – Yorkshire pudding, mustard and horseradish sauce – is still a favourite. The tougher cuts, which tend to be less expensive, make

Above *Beef has been associated with the English for centuries.*

delicious stews (with or without dumplings), pot roasts (such as boiled beef and carrots), and traditional puddings and pies, as well as the modern burger. The Victorians were great believers in the virtues of meat extracts, and invalids drank restorative "beef tea", made by simmering steak in water, cooling to remove all fat and residue and then reheated to serve.

Below *Oxtail is a very economical cut of beef, which needs slow cooking.*

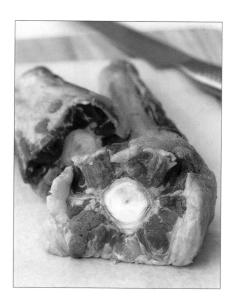

Above Curworthy.

Curworthy is a hard Devon cheese based on a 17th-century recipe and made from unpasteurized milk. It has a creamy yet open texture and a mild, buttery taste.

Devon Garland is an unpasteurized, semi-hard cheese made from the milk of (usually) Jersey cows. Its rind is firm and smooth with a greyish brown crust. A layer of fresh herbs is added before the cheese is matured.

Cotherstone comes from Yorkshire. It is an unpasteurized, hard cheese with a slight acidity and a fresh, citrus tang.

Below Stilton.

Blue cheeses

Stilton is historically referred to as "the king of cheeses". It has narrow, blue-green veins and a wrinkled rind, which is not edible. Its texture is smooth and creamy and its flavour is rich and mellow with a piquant aftertaste. It was never actually made in the village of Stilton, in Huntingdonshire, but was first sold there. The cheese originated at Quenby near Melton Mowbray in the early 18th century. Its certification trademark and Protected Designation of Origin status allows it to be made only in the counties of Nottinghamshire, Derbyshire, and Leicestershire, to a specified recipe. Crumble it over salads, cook with it or offer it as a dessert cheese. At Christmas Stilton is traditionally served with port. A white variety is also available.

Dorset Blue Vinney gets its name from an Old English word for mould. The popularity enjoyed by this cheese in the 18th and 19th centuries declined with the introduction of factory cheese-making, and it became extinct in the 1960s, but happily is now being made again. It is a hard cheese, light in texture with a mild flavour.

Beenleigh Blue is made in Devon from unpasteurized sheep's milk. The rough, crusty, natural rind is slightly sticky with patches of blue, grey and white moulds. It is moist and crumbly, with blue-green streaks through the white interior. It is good served with a glass of mead or sweet cider.

Shropshire Blue is not from Shropshire at all: having been invented in Scotland, it is now produced in Leicestershire. This distinctive orange-coloured cheese with its blue veins has a firm, creamy texture and a sharp, strong flavour. Eating Shropshire

Above Shropshire Blue.

Blue with a cup of tea is said to bring out its flavour.

Buxton Blue is a pale orange, lightly veined cheese. Appreciate its "blue" flavour in soups, salads or spread on crackers. It is perfect with chilled sweet dessert wine.

Oxford Blue was created less than 20 years ago as an alternative to Stilton. It is creamy with a distinct "blue" flavour and is sold wrapped in silver foil.

Dovedale is a creamy soft, mild blue cheese that has been dipped in brine. It is made in Derbyshire and takes its name from a beautiful valley in the Peak District.

Below Buxton Blue.

Eggs

Above *Eggs laid by free-range hens are now available everywhere in England.*

In the past, several types of eggs were eaten, most of which would have been smaller than today's. While hen's eggs have always been the most numerous, those from bantams, ducks and geese have been popular too. Peacock's eggs are known to have been an occasional luxury for the rich. Until the introduction of laws to protect wild birds; it was customary for the poor to plunder the nests of thrush, blackbird, mallard, moorhen, plover, seagull, sparrow and wood pigeon.

There was a time when most farms and households kept poultry for eggs, and also for meat. After the corn harvest the flocks of birds were driven to the fields to feed on the stubble and

Above *Hen's eggs.*

scattered grain. Eggs were once only a seasonal food, so they would be preserved for winter use: they were either waxed (coated with lard), pickled in brine or vinegar, or put in isinglass (or waterglass), a form of gelatine. In 1942, during the food shortages of World War II, dried eggs were introduced with an allocation of one tin (the equivalent of a dozen eggs) per person every 8 weeks.

Today, hens' eggs are available all year round. Though laying cages are still the most common method of commercial egg production, more and more are being supplied from barns and from free-range hens with daytime access to runs. Also available, in smaller numbers, are eggs from ducks (favoured by many for their stronger flavour), geese (a rich treat) and quail.

In Victorian times, eggs became a standard breakfast food, served boiled, poached, coddled, fried, rumbled (scrambled) or made into omelettes. These days they are an integral part of the traditional English breakfast, accompanied by bacon, sausages and other extras. Away from the breakfast table, eggs are used in numerous ways in English baking, to make cakes, puddings, flans, pancakes, sauces and

Above *Duck eggs have a richer flavour than hen's eggs, and are slightly larger.*

custards. Eggs are superb for quick, healthy light meals – a cheese omelette takes just minutes to make, as does fried or poached egg on toast. And no English picnic is complete without hardboiled eggs, peeled and dipped into salt and pepper.

Below *Little quail eggs make a very simple and attractive appetizer.*

Breakfasts

In medieval days the people of England simply ate bread and drank ale before a day in the fields. Over the centuries breakfast (or breaking the overnight fast) changed and, by the late 19th century, it was a more elaborate affair, with the tables of the wealthy laden with food. Such ostentation ended with two world wars, and a more seemly approach followed, with regional variations providing interest.

Omelette Arnold Bennett

This creamy, smoked haddock soufflé omelette was created for the post-theatre suppers of the famous English novelist, who frequently stayed at the Savoy Hotel in London after World War I. It is now served all over the world as a sustaining breakfast or supper dish.

Serves 2

175g/6oz smoked haddock fillet, poached and drained

50g/2oz butter, diced

175ml/6fl oz/¾ cup whipping or double (heavy) cream

4 eggs, separated

40g/1½oz mature (sharp) Cheddar cheese, grated

ground black pepper

watercress, to garnish

1 Remove and discard the skin and any bones from the haddock fillet by carefully pressing down the length of each fillet with your fingertips.

2 Using two forks and following the grain of the flesh, flake the fish into large chunks.

Cook's tip It's best to buy smoked haddock that does not contain artificial colouring for this recipe. Besides being better for you, it gives the omelette a better flavour and a lighter, more attractive colour.

3 Melt half the butter with 60ml/4 tbsp of the cream in a small non-stick pan. When the mixture is hot but not boiling, add the fish. Stir together gently, taking care not to break up the flakes of fish. Bring slowly to the boil, stirring continuously, then cover the pan, remove from the heat and set aside to cool for at least 20 minutes.

4 Preheat the grill (broiler) to high. Mix the egg yolks with 15ml/1 tbsp of the cream. Season with ground black pepper, then stir into the fish. In a separate bowl, mix the cheese and the remaining cream. Stiffly whisk the egg whites, then fold into the fish mixture.

5 Heat the remaining butter in an omelette pan until foaming. Add the fish mixture and cook until it is browned underneath. Pour the cheese mixture evenly over the top and grill (broil) until it is bubbling. Serve immediately, garnished with watercress.

Energy 821kcal/3396kj; Protein 36.1g; Carbohydrate 2.6g, of which sugars 2.6g; Fat 74g, of which saturates 42.6g; Cholesterol 577mg; Calcium 280mg; Fibre 0g; Sodium 1123mg.

Bubble and squeak

The name of this dish is derived from the noises the mixture makes as it cooks. Originally, it included chopped, boiled beef and was sprinkled with vinegar. This version is traditionally served with cold roast meat and pickles, but also goes very well with bacon and eggs.

Serves 4

60ml/4 tbsp oil

1 onion, finely chopped

450g/1lb cooked, mashed potatoes

225g/8oz cooked cabbage or Brussels sprouts, chopped

salt and ground black pepper

1 Heat half the oil in a heavy, preferably non-stick frying pan. Add the onion and cook, stirring frequently, until softened but not browned.

2 Mix together the mashed potatoes and cabbage or sprouts and season to taste with salt and plenty of pepper.

Cook's tips Though cabbage is traditional, other cooked vegetables could be added too.
• Using bacon fat or dripping in place of oil adds extra flavour.

3 Add the vegetable mixture to the pan, stir well to incorporate the cooked onions, then flatten the mixture out over the base of the pan to form a large, even cake.

4 Cook over a medium heat for about 15 minutes, until the cake is nicely browned underneath.

5 Hold a large plate over the pan, then invert the cake onto it. Add the remaining oil to the pan and, when hot, slip the cake back into the pan, browned side uppermost.

6 Continue cooking for about 10 minutes, until the underside is golden brown. Serve hot, cut into wedges.

Energy 219kcal/908kJ; Protein 2.5g; Carbohydrate 17.2g, of which sugars 2.5g; Fat 15.9g, of which saturates 1.9g; Cholesterol 0mg; Calcium 33mg; Fibre 2.6g; Sodium 14mg.

Full English breakfast

For most of us, a cooked breakfast is a special treat, harking back to the 19th century when the buffet tables of the rich groaned with food. As well as bacon, sausages and eggs cooked in a variety of ways, there might have been fish, kedgeree, potatoes, kidneys, chops, steaks, sliced cold meats and devilled chicken or pheasant to choose from.

Serves 4

225–250g/8–9oz small potatoes

oil, for grilling or frying

butter, for grilling and frying

4 large or 8 small good-quality sausages

8 rashers (strips) of back or streaky bacon, preferably dry-cured

4 tomatoes

4 small slices of bread, crusts removed

4 eggs

3 Meanwhile, grill or fry the sausages in a little oil until golden brown all over and cooked through (test by inserting a skewer in the centre – the juices should run clear). Keep warm.

4 Grill the bacon or fry it in a little oil in the non-stick pan. Keep warm.

1 Thinly slice the potatoes. Heat 15ml/ 1 tbsp oil with a knob of butter in a large, preferably non-stick frying pan, add the potatoes and cook over a medium heat for 10–15 minutes, turning them occasionally until they are crisp, golden, and cooked through.

2 Using a slotted spoon, lift the potatoes out of the pan and keep them warm on a dish in a low oven.

Cook's tip For the best flavour, fry the bread and tomatoes in the fatty juices remaining in the pan from the sausages and bacon.

5 Halve the tomatoes and either top each half with a tiny piece of butter and grill until they are soft and bubbling, or fry in a little oil in the frying pan. Keep warm.

6 Fry the bread in a little oil and butter over a medium-high heat until crisp and golden brown. Keep warm.

7 Add extra oil if necessary to the hot frying pan. As soon as the oil is hot, crack the eggs into the pan, leaving space between them. Cook over a medium heat, spooning the hot fat over occasionally to set the yolks, until cooked to your liking.

8 As soon as the eggs are cooked to your liking, arrange the breakfast ingredients on warmed plates and serve immediately.

Variations English cafés often serve breakfast in a roll – warm a long crusty rolls in the oven, then cut them in half vertically without slicing through the bottom crust. Fill each roll with the hot breakfast ingredients, draping the fried egg over the top. Serve with a serrated knife for cutting.
• Slices of black pudding (blood sausage) can be gently fried or grilled and served in place of the sausages.
• A few field mushrooms fried in the fat left in the pan after cooking the bacon make a delicious addition to a traditional English breakfast.
• Serve a spoonful of bubble and squeak in place of the fried potatoes.

Energy 731kcal/3046kJ; Protein 32.7g; Carbohydrate 35.3g, of which sugars 7.6g; Fat 52.2g, of which saturates 16.5g; Cholesterol 288mg; Calcium 185mg; Fibre 3.1g; Sodium 2049mg.

Scrambled eggs

Carefully cooked scrambled eggs are deliciously comforting. They cook best in a pan with a heavy base. Serve them on hot buttered toast or with bacon, sausages or smoked fish.

Serves 2

4 eggs

25g/1oz butter

salt and ground black pepper

1 Break the eggs into a bowl and beat lightly with a fork until well mixed. Season with salt and pepper.

2 Put a medium-sized heavy pan over a medium heat and add half the butter. When the butter begins to foam, add the beaten eggs. Using a wooden spoon, stir the eggs constantly as they cook and thicken, making sure you get right into the angle of the pan to prevent the eggs sticking there and overcooking.

3 When the eggs are quite thick and beginning to set, but still creamy, remove the pan from the heat and stir in the remaining butter. The eggs will finish cooking gently in the residual heat of the pan as you keep stirring. When they are set to your liking, serve immediately.

Poached egg

This delicate method of cooking eggs has been popular in England since the Middle Ages. Use poaching rings in the water if you have them for a perfect shape. Only use fresh eggs.

Serves 2

2–4 eggs

1 Put a frying pan over a medium heat and add 5cm/2in of boiling water. Add the poaching rings if you have them.

2 When tiny bubbles begin to gather in the water and gently rise to the surface, break the eggs, one at a time, into a cup and slide them carefully into the hot water. Leave the pan on the heat for 1 minute as the water simmers very gently (on no account allow it to boil). Then remove from the heat and leave the eggs to stand, uncovered, in the hot water for 10 minutes.

3 Use a slotted spoon to lift the eggs out of the water and drain briefly on kitchen paper. Serve immediately with toasted muffins.

Cook's tip Poaching pans are available with little cups for the eggs.

Energy 240kcal/995kJ; Protein 12.6g; Carbohydrate 0.1g, of which sugars 0.1g; Fat 21.4g, of which saturates 9.6g; Cholesterol 407mg; Calcium 60mg; Fibre 0g; Sodium 216mg

Energy 74kcal/306kJ; Protein 6.3g; Carbohydrate 0g, of which sugars 0g; Fat 5.6g, of which saturates 1.6g; Cholesterol 190mg; Calcium 29mg; Fibre 0g; Sodium 70mg.

Boiled egg

Soft-boiled eggs are just made for dipping bread or toast "soldiers". In summer, they also make a delicious accompaniment to freshly cooked asparagus spears.

Serves 2

2–4 eggs

hot buttered toast, to serve

1 Put the eggs into a pan just large enough to hold them in a single layer and cover with cold water. Bring to the boil, then simmer for 3 minutes for soft-boiled, 4 minutes for a just-set yolk, or 8 minutes for hard-boiled.

2 Drain and serve immediately with hot buttered toast.

Cook's tip
To ensure the eggs do not crack during cooking, prick a tiny hole in the round end (where there is a pocket of air).

Coddled eggs

This method of soft-cooking eggs became very popular in the Victorian era, and special decorative porcelain pots with lids were produced by Royal Worcester from the 1890s.

Serves 2

butter, for greasing

2 large eggs

60ml/4 tbsp single (light) cream (optional)

chopped fresh chives, to garnish

1 Butter two small ramekin dishes or cups and break an egg into each. Top with a spoonful of cream, if using, and a knob of butter. Cover with foil.

2 Put a wide, shallow pan over medium heat. Stand the covered dishes in the pan. Add boiling water to come half way up the sides of the dishes.

3 Heat until the water just comes to the boil then cover the pan with a lid and simmer gently for 1 minute.

4 Remove from the heat and leave to stand, still covered, for 10 minutes. Serve sprinkled with chives.

Energy 74kcal/306kJ; Protein 6.3g; Carbohydrate 0g, of which sugars 0g; Fat 5.6g, of which saturates 1.6g; Cholesterol 190mg; Calcium 29mg; Fibre 0g; Sodium 70mg.

Energy 92kcal/383kJ; Protein 6.3g; Carbohydrate 0g, of which sugars 0g; Fat 7.6g, of which saturates 2.9g; Cholesterol 196mg; Calcium 29mg; Fibre 0g; Sodium 85mg.

Gateshead bacon floddies

This Tyneside breakfast special is traditionally cooked in bacon fat and served with eggs and sausages. A kind of potato cake, floddies are said to have originated with canal workers, who cooked them on shovels over a fire. They should be served crisp and golden brown.

Serves 4–6

250g/9oz potatoes, weighed after peeling

1 large onion

175g/6oz rindless streaky (fat) bacon, finely chopped

50g/2oz/½ cup self-raising (self-rising) flour

2 eggs

oil, for frying

salt and ground black pepper

Cook's tip
Fry the floddies in oiled metal rings if you wish, for a neat circular shape.

1 Grate the potatoes onto a clean dish cloth, and then gather up the edges to make a pouch. Squeeze and twist the towel to remove the liquid.

2 Grate or finely chop the onion into a mixing bowl and add the potatoes, chopped bacon, flour and seasoning, mixing well.

3 Beat the eggs and stir into the potato mixture. Heat some oil in a large frying pan. Add generous tablespoonfuls of the potato mixture to the hot oil and flatten them to make thin cakes. Cook over a medium heat for 3–4 minutes on each side or until golden brown and cooked through. Lift out, drain on kitchen paper and serve.

Energy 214kcal/891kJ; Protein 8.8g; Carbohydrate 17.1g, of which sugars 3.5g; Fat 12.7g, of which saturates 3.4g; Cholesterol 82mg; Calcium 38mg; Fibre 1.4g; Sodium 397mg.

Mushrooms on toast

Cultivated or wild mushrooms make a delicious addition to a full English breakfast. They also make a meaty treat when cooked with cream and served on toast. For the best flavour and texture, cook them quickly and serve without delay.

Serves 2

250g/9oz button (white) or closed-cup mushrooms

5ml/1 tsp oil

15g/½oz butter, plus extra for spreading

60ml/4 tbsp double (heavy) cream

freshly grated nutmeg

2 thick slices of bread

chopped chives or parsley, to garnish

salt and ground black pepper

1 Pick over and trim the mushrooms and cut into thick slices.

2 Heat the oil and butter in a non-stick pan, add the sliced mushrooms and cook quickly for about 3 minutes, stirring frequently.

3 Stir in the cream and season with salt, pepper and a little nutmeg. Simmer for 1–2 minutes.

4 Toast the bread and spread with butter. Top with the mushrooms, sprinkle with chopped herbs and serve.

Energy 350kcal/1460kJ; Protein 6.8g; Carbohydrate 25.7g, of which sugars 2.1g; Fat 25.3g, of which saturates 14.2g; Cholesterol 57mg; Calcium 78mg; Fibre 2g; Sodium 318mg.

Grilled kippers with marmalade toast

Wonderful kippers are produced around the English coast, in places such as East Anglia and Craster in Northumberland, where the herrings are still cured in the traditional smokehouses that were erected in the mid-19th century. In this recipe the smokiness of the kipper is complemented with the tang of orange marmalade.

Serves 2

melted butter, for greasing

2 kippers

2 slices of bread

soft butter, for spreading

orange marmalade, for spreading

Variation Omit the marmalade and cook the kippers sprinkled with a little cayenne pepper. Serve with a knob of butter and plenty of lemon wedges for squeezing over.

1 Preheat the grill (broiler). Line the grill pan with foil – to help prevent fishy smells from lingering in the pan – and brush the foil with melted butter to stop the fish sticking.

2 Using kitchen scissors, or a knife, cut the heads and tails off the kippers.

3 Lay the fish, skin side up, on the buttered foil. Put under the hot grill and cook for 1 minute. Turn the kippers over, brush the uppermost (fleshy) side with melted butter, put back under the grill and cook for 4–5 minutes.

4 Toast the bread and spread it first with butter and then with marmalade. Serve the sizzling hot kippers immediately with the marmalade toast.

Energy 518kcal/2155kJ; Protein 33.9g; Carbohydrate 17.6g, of which sugars 5.9g; Fat 35.1g, of which saturates 7.6g; Cholesterol 121mg; Calcium 126mg; Fibre 0.4g; Sodium 1640mg

Kedgeree

Introduced from British-ruled India, kedgeree became popular in 18th-century England, when the original Hindi dish of rice, lentils and onion (*khitchri*) was adapted to English tastes by the addition of flaked smoked fish and hard-boiled eggs. While it is traditionally served for breakfast, this also makes a delicious lunch or supper dish.

Serves 4–6

450g/1lb smoked haddock

300ml/½ pint/1¼ cups milk

175g/6oz/scant 1 cup long-grain rice

pinch each of grated nutmeg and cayenne pepper

50g/2oz butter

1 onion, finely chopped

2 hard-boiled eggs, shelled

chopped fresh parsley, to garnish

lemon wedges and wholemeal (whole-wheat) toast, to serve

salt and ground black pepper

1 Gently poach the haddock in the milk, made up with just enough water to cover the fish, for about 8 minutes, or until just cooked. Lift out. Skin the haddock, remove all the bones and flake the fish with a fork. Set aside.

2 Bring 600ml/1 pint/2½ cups water to the boil in a large pan. Add the rice, cover closely with a lid and cook over a low heat for about 25 minutes, or until all the water has been absorbed by the rice. Season with salt and black pepper, nutmeg and cayenne pepper.

3 Meanwhile, heat 15g/½oz butter in a pan and fry the onion until soft and transparent. Set aside. Roughly chop one of the hard-boiled eggs and cut the other into neat wedges.

4 Stir the remaining butter into the hot rice and add the flaked haddock, onion and the chopped egg. Season to taste and heat the mixture through gently, stirring constantly.

5 To serve, pile the kedgeree onto a warmed dish, sprinkle generously with parsley and arrange the wedges of egg on top. Garnish with lemon wedges and serve hot with toast.

Variation Try using the same quantity of cooked salmon in place of the smoked haddock.

Energy 320kcal/1337kJ; Protein 15.6g; Carbohydrate 46.6g, of which sugars 0g; Fat 7.6g, of which saturates 3.2g; Cholesterol 149mg; Calcium 39mg; Fibre 0g; Sodium 357mg.

Soups and Appetizers

Soups have always been a staple food in England – from a thin pottage of onions, wild plants and cereals, through scraps-thrown-in-the-pot soup dished out to the poor, to elegant concoctions eaten by the wealthy in preparation for courses to come. Today, winter or summer, delicate or substantial, there is a soup for every occasion. Other savoury dishes whet the appetite with local ingredients and exotic imports.

Cream of tomato soup

When the tomato first came to England it was thought to be an aphrodisiac, and until the late 19th century it was viewed with great suspicion in case it caused sickness. When it was used, it was usually cooked in soups and stews, and was rarely eaten raw. This creamy soup owes its good flavour to a mix of fresh and canned tomatoes – in summer you could, of course, use all fresh, but do make sure they are really ripe and full of flavour.

Serves 4–6

25g/1oz/2 tbsp butter

1 medium onion, finely chopped

1 small carrot, finely chopped

1 celery stick, finely chopped

1 garlic clove, crushed

450g/1lb ripe tomatoes, roughly chopped

400g/14oz can chopped tomatoes

30ml/2 tbsp tomato purée (paste)

30ml/2 tbsp sugar

1 tbsp chopped fresh thyme or oregano leaves

600ml/1 pint/2½ cups chicken or vegetable stock

600ml/1 pint/2½ cups milk

salt and ground black pepper

1 Melt the butter in a large pan. Add the onion, carrot, celery and garlic. Cook over a medium heat for about 5 minutes, stirring occasionally, until soft and just beginning to brown.

2 Add the tomatoes, purée, sugar, stock and herbs, retaining some to garnish.

3 Bring to the boil, then cover and simmer gently for about 20 minutes until all the vegetables are very soft.

4 Process or blend the mixture until smooth, then press it through a sieve (strainer) to remove the skins and seeds.

5 Return the sieved soup to the cleaned pan and stir in the milk. Reheat gently.

6 Stir, without allowing it to boil. Season to taste with salt and ground black pepper. Garnish with the remaining herbs and serve.

Energy 107kcal/447kJ; Protein 2.3g; Carbohydrate 11.4g, of which sugars 10.9g; Fat 6.1g, of which saturates 3.5g; Cholesterol 13mg; Calcium 50mg; Fibre 3.9g; Sodium 71mg.

Jerusalem artichoke soup

Related to the sunflower and also known as root artichoke or sunchoke, Jerusalem artichoke was introduced to England in the 17th century. At first it was prized but then became so common an ingredient that people began to lose their taste for it. The tubers can be knobbly, choose those with a fairly smooth surface for easier cleaning or peeling. Roasting the artichokes before making this soup brings out their sweet, nutty flavour.

Serves 4–6

500g/1¼lb Jerusalem artichokes

1 onion, roughly chopped

4 celery sticks, roughly chopped

2 carrots, roughly chopped

4 garlic cloves

45ml/3 tbsp olive oil

1.2 litre/2 pints/5 cups vegetable or chicken stock

60ml/4 tbsp double (heavy) cream

salt and ground black pepper

1 Preheat the oven to 200°C/400°F/Gas 6. Scrub the artichokes well and halve them lengthways.

2 Toss all the vegetables in the olive oil and spread them in a roasting pan.

3 Put the vegetables into the hot oven and roast for 30–40 minutes until they are soft and golden brown. Stir them once during cooking so that the edges brown evenly.

4 Tip the roasted vegetables into a large pan.

Cook's tip Peel the artichokes before roasting, if preferred, dropping them into water with a good squeeze of lemon to prevent them discolouring once peeled.

5 Add the stock, bring to the boil and simmer for 15 minutes. Process or blend until smooth, return to the pan, add the cream, season, and reheat gently.

Energy 310kcal/1277kJ; Protein 2.7g; Carbohydrate 4.7g, of which sugars 4.3g; Fat 31.3g, of which saturates 19.4g; Cholesterol 80mg; Calcium 116mg; Fibre 1.5g; Sodium 168mg

Watercress soup

In Roman times, eating watercress was thought to prevent baldness. Later on it became the food of the working classes and was often eaten for breakfast in a sandwich. Watercress has been cultivated in the south of England since the early 19th century. Both stalks and leaves are used in this soup for a lovely peppery flavour.

2 Melt the butter in a large pan and add the onion. Cook over a medium heat for about 5 minutes, stirring occasionally, until the onion is soft and just beginning to brown.

3 Stir in the potato and the chopped watercress, then add the stock. Bring to the boil, cover the pan and simmer gently for 15–20 minutes until the potato is very soft.

4 Remove from the heat, leave to cool slightly and then stir in the milk.

5 Process or blend the mixture until the soup is completely smooth.

6 Return the soup to the pan and adjust the seasoning to taste.

7 Reheat gently and top each serving with a spoonful of cream and a few watercress leaves.

Serves 6

2 bunches of watercress, about 175g/6oz in total

25g/1oz/2 tbsp butter

1 medium onion, finely chopped

1 medium potato

900ml/1½ pints/3¾ cups chicken or vegetable stock

300ml/½ pint/1¼ cups milk

salt and ground black pepper

single (light) cream, to serve

1 Roughly chop the watercress, reserving a few small sprigs to garnish.

Cook's tip Try adding a little finely grated orange rind and the juice of an orange in step 6.

Energy 68kcal/280kJ; Protein 1.5g; Carbohydrate 1.4g, of which sugars 1g; Fat 6.3g, of which saturates 2.4g; Cholesterol 8mg; Calcium 79mg; Fibre 0.9g; Sodium 45mg

Country vegetable soup

Vegetable soups have always been particularly popular in the north of England. In the reign of Victoria, during extreme food shortages, vegetable soup kitchens were opened in Manchester. Soup-making is a good way to make the most of seasonal vegetables. Serve this one as an appetizer or with crusty bread and perhaps a wedge of cheese as a light meal.

Serves 6

15ml/1 tbsp oil

25g/1oz/2 tbsp butter

2 medium onions, finely chopped

4 medium carrots, sliced

2 celery sticks, sliced

2 leeks, sliced

1 potato, cut into small cubes

1 small parsnip, cut into small cubes

1 garlic clove, crushed

900ml/1½ pints/3¾ cups vegetable stock

300ml/½ pint/1¼ cups milk

25g/1oz/4 tbsp cornflour (cornstarch)

handful of frozen peas

30ml/2 tbsp chopped fresh parsley

salt and ground black pepper

2 Add the stock to the pan and stir into the vegetables. Bring the mixture slowly to the boil, cover and simmer gently for 20–30 minutes until all the vegetables are soft.

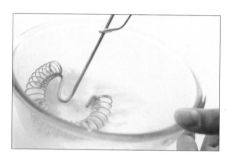

3 Whisk the milk into the cornflour, making a paste. Stir into the vegetables. Add the frozen peas. Bring to the boil and simmer for 5 minutes Adjust the seasoning, stir in the parsley and serve.

1 Heat the oil and butter in a large pan and add the onions, carrots and celery. Cook over a medium heat for 5–10 minutes, stirring occasionally, until soft and just beginning to turn golden brown. Stir in the leeks, potato, parsnip and garlic.

Energy 160kcal/665kJ; Protein 3.6g; Carbohydrate 11.5g, of which sugars 10g; Fat 11.4g, of which saturates 6.8g; Cholesterol 27mg; Calcium 72mg; Fibre 5.4g; Sodium 106mg

Celery soup with stilton

Stilton – known as the "king of English cheeses" – and celery are traditional partners, whether on the cheeseboard or in this warming winter soup. The two flavours complement each other beautifully, with the fresh, clean taste of the celery setting off the rich, creamy texture and tang of the famous blue-veined cheese.

3 Add the stock, bring to the boil, then cover the pan and simmer gently for about 30 minutes, until all the vegetables are very soft.

4 Process or blend about three-quarters of the mixture until smooth, then return it to the pan with the rest of the soup.

5 Bring the soup just to the boil and season to taste with salt and ground black pepper.

6 Remove the pan from the heat and stir in the cheese, reserving a little for the garnish. Stir in the cream and reheat the soup gently without boiling.

7 Serve topped with the reserved crumbled cheese.

Serves 6

40g/1½oz/3 tbsp butter

1 large onion, finely chopped

1 medium potato, cut into small cubes

1 whole head of celery, thinly sliced

900ml/1½ pints/3¾ cups vegetable or chicken stock

100g/3¾oz Stilton cheese, crumbled

150ml/¼ pint/⅔ cup single (light) cream

salt and ground black pepper

1 Melt the butter in a large pan and add the onion. Cook over a medium heat for 5 minutes, stirring occasionally, until soft but not browned.

2 Stir in the potato and celery and cook for a further 5 minutes until the vegetables soften and begin to brown.

Cook's tip In the place of Stilton try using another cheese, either a blue-veined variety or a strong Cheddar.

Energy 199kcal/826kJ; Protein 5.9g; Carbohydrate 7.5g, of which sugars 2.4g; Fat 16.2g, of which saturates 10.4g; Cholesterol 44mg; Calcium 117mg; Fibre 1.4g; Sodium 233mg

Parsnip and apple soup

The Romans introduced apple orchards to England. Since then the country has been proud of its wonderful range of apples, and many fine apple juices are now available, often made from single varieties. For this soup, choose a fairly sharp-tasting juice – it will complement the sweetness of the parsnips and the warmth of the spices.

Serves 4–6

25g/1oz/2 tbsp butter

1 medium onion, finely chopped

1 garlic clove, finely chopped

500g/1¼lb parsnips, peeled and thinly sliced

5ml/1 tsp curry paste or powder

300ml/½ pint/1¼ cups apple juice

600ml/1 pint/2½ cups vegetable stock

300ml/½ pint/1¼ cups milk

salt and ground black pepper

thick natural yogurt, to serve

chopped fresh herbs such as mint or parsley, to serve

1 Melt the butter in a large pan and add the onion, garlic and parsnips. Cook gently, without browning, for about 10 minutes, stirring often.

2 Add the curry paste or powder and cook, stirring, for 1 minute.

Variation This recipe is also delicious when the parsnips are replaced with butternut squash or an equal mixture of the two.

3 Add the juice and stock, bring to the boil, cover and simmer gently for about 20 minutes until the parsnips are soft.

4 Process or blend the mixture until smooth and return it to the pan.

5 Add the milk and season to taste with salt and pepper.

6 Reheat the soup gently and serve topped with a spoonful of yogurt and a sprinkling of herbs.

Energy 130kcal/548kJ; Protein 3.4g; Carbohydrate 18.5g, of which sugars 12.6g; Fat 5.3g, of which saturates 2.9g; Cholesterol 12mg; Calcium 101mg; Fibre 4g; Sodium 56mg

Shropshire pea and mint soup

Peas have been grown in England since the Middle Ages, while mint was made popular by the Romans. Peas and mint picked fresh from the garden are still true seasonal treats and make a velvety, fresh-tasting soup. When fresh peas are out of season, use frozen peas.

Serves 6

25g/1oz/2 tbsp butter

1 medium onion, finely chopped

675g/1½lb shelled fresh peas

1.5ml/¼ tsp sugar

1.2 litres/2 pints/5 cups chicken or vegetable stock

handful of fresh mint leaves

150ml/¼ pint/⅔ cup double (heavy) cream

salt and ground black pepper

snipped fresh chives, to serve

1 Melt the butter in a large pan and add the onion. Cook over a low heat for about 10 minutes, stirring occasionally, until soft and just brown.

2 Add the peas, sugar, stock and half the mint. Cover and simmer gently for 10–15 minutes until the peas are tender.

3 Leave to cool slightly. Add the remaining mint and process or blend until smooth. Return the soup to the pan and season to taste.

4 Stir in the cream and reheat gently without boiling. Serve garnished with snipped chives.

Energy 121kcal/506kJ; Protein 6.1g; Carbohydrate 9.2g, of which sugars 5.2g; Fat 7g, of which saturates 4.2g; Cholesterol 18mg; Calcium 113mg; Fibre 3g; Sodium 123mg

London particular

Victorian London was regularly covered with a thick winter fog, known as a "pea-souper", or "London particular", because it had the colour and consistency of pea soup. The original version of this soup would probably have included pig's trotters and a marrow bone.

Serves 4–6

350g/12oz/1½ cups dried split yellow or green peas

25g/1oz/2 tbsp butter

6 rashers (strips) rindless lean streaky (fatty) bacon, finely chopped

1 medium onion, finely chopped

1 medium carrot, thinly sliced

1 celery stick, thinly sliced

1.75 litres/3 pints/7½ cups ham or chicken stock

60ml/4 tbsp double (heavy) cream

salt and ground black pepper

croûtons and fried bacon, to serve

1 Put the split peas into a large bowl, cover well with boiling water (from the kettle) and leave to stand.

2 Meanwhile, melt the butter in a large pan. Add the bacon, onion, carrot and celery and cook over a medium heat for 10–15 minutes, stirring occasionally until the vegetables are soft and beginning to turn golden brown.

3 Drain the peas and add them to the pan. Stir in the stock. Bring to the boil, cover and simmer gently for about 1 hour or until the peas are very soft.

4 Process or blend until smooth and return the soup to the pan. Season to taste and stir in the cream. Heat until just bubbling and serve with croûtons and pieces of crisp bacon on top.

Energy 378kcal/1584kJ; Protein 20.2g; Carbohydrate 34.9g, of which sugars 3.1g; Fat 18.5g, of which saturates 8.7g; Cholesterol 47mg; Calcium 45mg; Fibre 3.4g; Sodium 527mg

Oxtail soup

This hearty soup is an English classic, stemming from the days when it was natural to make use of every part of an animal. Oxtail may start off tough and full of bone, but long slow cooking produces a flavour that is rich and delicious, and meat that is beautifully tender.

Serves 4–6

1 oxtail, cut into joints, total weight about 1.3kg/3lb

25g/1oz/2 tbsp butter

2 medium onions, chopped

2 medium carrots, chopped

2 celery sticks, sliced

1 bacon rasher (strip), chopped

2 litres/3½ pints/8 cups beef stock

1 bouquet garni

2 bay leaves

30ml/2 tbsp flour

squeeze of fresh lemon juice

60ml/4 tbsp port, sherry or Madeira

salt and ground black pepper

1 Wash and dry the pieces of oxtail, trimming off any excess fat. Melt the butter in a large pan, and when foaming, add the oxtail a few pieces at a time and brown them quickly on all sides. Lift the meat out onto a plate.

2 To the same pan, add the onions, carrots, celery and bacon. Cook over a medium heat for 5–10 minutes, stirring occasionally, until the vegetables are softened and golden brown.

3 Return the oxtail to the pan and add the stock, bouquet garni, bay leaves and seasoning. Bring just to the boil and skim off any foam. Cover and simmer gently for about 3 hours or until the meat is so tender that it is falling away from the bones.

4 Strain the mixture, discarding the vegetables, bouquet garni and bay leaves, and leave to stand.

5 When the oxtail has cooled sufficiently to handle, pick all the meat off the bones and cut it into small pieces.

6 Skim off any fat that has risen to the surface of the stock, then tip the stock into a large pan. Add the pieces of meat and reheat.

7 With a whisk, blend the flour with a little cold water to make a smooth paste. Stir in a little of the hot stock then stir the mixture into the pan. Bring to the boil, stirring, until the soup thickens slightly. Reduce the heat and simmer gently for about 5 minutes.

8 Season with salt, pepper and lemon juice to taste. Just before serving, stir in the port, sherry or Madeira.

Energy 459kcal/1914kJ; Protein 45.4g; Carbohydrate 6.5g, of which sugars 2.6g; Fat 26.8g, of which saturates 11.8g; Cholesterol 176mg; Calcium 36mg; Fibre 0.7g; Sodium 403mg

Brown Windsor soup

Another classic hearty soup, this was particularly popular during the reign of Queen Victoria, when it is said to have featured regularly on state banquet menus at Windsor Castle in Berkshire. It is smooth, meaty, full of flavour and pleasantly substantial.

Serves 4

225g/8oz lean stewing steak

30ml/2 tbsp flour

25g/1oz/2 tbsp butter

1 medium onion, finely chopped

1 medium carrot, finely chopped

1 small parsnip, finely chopped

1 litre/1¾ pints/4 cups beef stock

1 bouquet garni

salt, black pepper and chilli powder

cooked rice, to garnish

3 Add the vegetables to the hot pan and cook over a medium heat for about 5 minutes, stirring occasionally until softened and golden brown.

4 Return the steak to the pan and add the stock, bouquet garni and seasoning.

5 Bring just to the boil, cover and simmer very gently for about 2 hours until the steak is very tender.

6 Process or blend the soup until smooth, adding a little extra hot stock or water to thin it if necessary. Return it to the pan, adjust the seasoning to taste and reheat. When the soup is in the serving bowls, add a spoonful of cooked rice to each one.

1 Cut the stewing steak into 2.5cm/1in cubes and coat with the flour.

2 Melt the butter in a large saucepan. Add the steak a few pieces at a time and brown them on all sides. Lift the meat out and set aside.

Energy 182kcal/757kJ; Protein 13.8g; Carbohydrate 8g, of which sugars 3.4g; Fat 10.7g, of which saturates 5.5g; Cholesterol 46mg; Calcium 25mg; Fibre 1.7g; Sodium 81mg

Pears with stilton, cream and walnuts

English cheeses and fruit taste wonderful together, as in traditional combinations such as apple pie with Wensleydale or Cheshire cheese with fruit cake. This dish needs pears that are fully ripe and juicy, yet firm – Comice, Conference or Williams all work well.

Serves 6

115g/4oz/½ cup cream cheese or curd cheese

75g/3oz Stilton cheese

30–45ml/2–3 tbsp single (light) cream

115g/4oz/1 cup roughly chopped walnuts

6 ripe pears

15ml/1 tbsp lemon juice

mixed salad leaves

6 cherry tomatoes

salt and ground black pepper

walnut halves and sprigs of fresh flat-leaf parsley, to garnish

For the dressing

juice of 1 lemon

a little finely grated lemon rind

pinch of caster (superfine) sugar

60ml/4 tbsp olive oil

2 Peel and halve the pears lengthways and scoop out the cores. Put them into a bowl of cold water with the lemon juice to prevent them from browning. Whisk the dressing ingredients together and season to taste.

3 Divide the salad leaves between six plates – shallow soup plates are ideal – add a tomato to each and sprinkle over the remaining chopped walnuts.

4 Drain the pears well and pat dry with kitchen paper, then turn them in the prepared dressing and arrange, hollow side up, on the salad. Pile the cheese mixture into the pears and spoon over the rest of the dressing. Garnish with walnut halves and flat leaf parsley.

Variation Try other blue cheeses such as Beenleigh Blue or Oxford Blue, or for a milder taste use soft cream cheese.

1 Mash the cream cheese and Stilton together with a good grinding of black pepper, then blend in the cream to make a smooth mixture. Stir in 25g/1oz/¼ cup chopped walnuts. Cover the mixture and chill until required.

Energy 407kcal/1684kJ; Protein 7.1g; Carbohydrate 16.7g, of which sugars 16.6g; Fat 34.9g, of which saturates 11.3g; Cholesterol 33mg; Calcium 100mg; Fibre 4.1g; Sodium 164mg

Potted cheese

The potting of cheese became popular in the 18th century, and it is still a great way to use up odd pieces left on the cheeseboard. Blend them with your chosen seasonings, adjusting the flavour before adding the alcohol. Serve with plain crackers, oatcakes or crisp toast.

Serves 4–6

250g/9oz hard cheese, such as mature Cheddar

75g/3oz/6 tbsp soft unsalted butter, plus extra for melting

1.5ml/¼ tsp ready-made English (hot) mustard

1.5ml/¼ tsp ground mace

30ml/2 tbsp sherry

ground black pepper

fresh parsley, to garnish

1 Cut the cheese into rough pieces and put them into the bowl of a food processor. Use the pulse button to chop the cheese into small crumbs.

2 Add the butter, mustard, mace and a little black pepper and blend again until smooth. Taste and adjust the seasoning. Finally, blend in the sherry.

3 Spoon the mixture into a dish just large enough to leave about 1cm/½in to spare on top. Level the surface.

Variations Use some crumbled Stilton in place of the Cheddar and the same quantity of port in place of sherry.
• Some finely chopped chives could be added instead of mustard.

4 Melt some butter in a small pan, skimming off any foam that rises to the surface. Leaving the sediment in the pan, pour a layer of melted butter on top of the cheese mixture to cover the surface. Refrigerate until required.

5 Garnish with parsley and serve spread on thin slices of toast or crispbread.

Energy 262kcal/1082kJ; Protein 10.7g; Carbohydrate 0.2g, of which sugars 0.2g; Fat 23.6g, of which saturates 15.2g; Cholesterol 70mg; Calcium 290mg; Fibre 0g; Sodium 363mg

Fish and Shellfish

England has always enjoyed wonderful fish and shellfish from its coastlines, lakes and rivers. It has a proud history of smokeries dedicated to preserving fresh fish – herrings and mackerel in particular. Cooking methods vary from simple pan-frying, steaming and baking, to delicious soups, sauces, casseroles, pies and fishcakes. And let's not forget the favourite national dish of fish and chips!

Poached salmon with hollandaise sauce

Though it was once plentiful, wild salmon is now a rare and expensive treat. These days farmed salmon is readily available and an economical choice. A whole poached fish makes an elegant party dish and served cold it is perfect for a summer buffet.

Serves 8–10

300ml/½ pint/1¼ cups dry (hard) cider or white wine

1 large carrot, roughly chopped

2 medium onions, roughly chopped

2 celery sticks, roughly chopped

2 bay leaves

a few black peppercorns

sprig of parsley

sprig of thyme

2–2.5kg/4½–5½lb whole salmon, gutted, washed and dried

For the hollandaise sauce

175g/6oz/¾ cup unsalted butter

5ml/1 tsp sugar

3 egg yolks

10ml/2 tsp cider vinegar or white wine vinegar

10ml/2 tsp lemon juice

salt and ground white pepper

1 Put all the ingredients except the salmon into a large pan and add 1 litre/1¾ pints/4 cups water. Bring to the boil and simmer gently for 30–40 minutes. Strain and leave to cool.

2 About 30 minutes before serving, pour the cooled stock into a fish kettle. Lay the salmon on the rack and lower it into the liquid.

3 Slowly heat the kettle until the stock almost comes to the boil (with small bubbles forming and rising to the surface), cover and simmer very gently for 20–25 minutes until the fish is just cooked through – test the thickest part with a knife near the backbone.

4 Meanwhile, to make the hollandaise sauce, heat the butter with the sugar (on the stove or in the microwave) until the butter has melted and the mixture is hot but not sizzling – do not allow it to brown.

5 Put the egg yolks, vinegar, lemon juice and seasonings into a processor or blender and blend on high speed for about 15 seconds, or until the mixture is creamy.

6 Keep the processor or blender on high speed and add the hot butter mixture in a slow stream until the sauce is thick, smooth and creamy.

7 Lift the salmon out of its cooking liquid. Remove the skin carefully, so the flesh remains intact, and lift the salmon on to a warmed serving plate. Garnish with watercress and serve with the warm hollandaise.

Variation To cook salmon that is to be served cold, in step 3 slowly heat until the stock just comes to the boil, let it bubble two or three times then cover, remove from the heat and leave to cool completely (this will take up to 12 hours). When cold, lift out the fish and slide it on to a serving plate. Strip off the fins and peel away the skin and garnish with wafer-thin cucumber slices arranged like scales, salad leaves, baby tomatoes or black olives. Serve the salmon with mayonnaise.

Energy 450kcal/1868kJ; Protein 34.6g; Carbohydrate 0.5g, of which sugars 0.5g; Fat 34.4g, of which saturates 12.8g; Cholesterol 182mg; Calcium 44mg; Fibre 0g; Sodium 183mg

Soused herrings

Cooking then storing fish in vinegar, or sousing, was a way to preserve the plentiful supplies of herring caught in the east of England, where these fish were a staple food.

Serves 4

4 large or 8 small filleted herrings

1 medium onion

200ml/7fl oz/scant 1 cup malt vinegar

5ml/1 tsp sugar

6 black peppercorns

2 bay leaves

2.5ml/½ tsp mustard seeds

2.5ml/½ tsp coriander seeds

pinch of ground ginger

1 small dried chilli

salt and ground black pepper

1 Preheat the oven to 150°C/300°F/ Gas 2. Lay out the herring fillets skin side down, and sprinkle the flesh with a little salt and pepper. Roll up the fillets from the head end and secure each one with a wooden cocktail stick or toothpick. Slice the onion horizontally and separate into thin rings.

2 Cover the bottom of a shallow ovenproof dish with a layer of onion rings, arrange the rolled herrings on top and scatter the remaining onion rings over them.

3 Mix the vinegar with 200ml/7fl oz/ scant 1 cup water and pour over the herrings. Add the remaining ingredients to the dish and cover securely with a lid or a sheet of foil.

4 Put into the preheated oven and cook for 1–1¼ hours or until the herrings are cooked through and the onion is very soft.

5 Leave the herrings to cool completely in the cooking liquid before serving.

Variations Use 7.5–10ml/1½–2 tsp ready-made pickling spice in place of the final six ingredients.
• Replace the vinegar and water with 400ml/14fl oz/1⅔ cups dry (hard) cider for a fruitier, less sharp flavour.

Energy 332kcal/1384kJ; Protein 30.5g; Carbohydrate 2.2g, of which sugars 1.9g; Fat 22.5g, of which saturates 5.6g; Cholesterol 85mg; Calcium 106mg; Fibre 0.2g; Sodium 205mg

Trout with almonds

The shallow streams and rivers of southern England once supplied an abundance of wild trout. Their earthy flavour goes particularly well with buttery juices and toasted almonds.

Serves 4

4 whole trout, cleaned

45–60ml/3–4 tbsp seasoned flour,

75g/3oz/6 tbsp butter

15ml/1 tbsp olive oil

50g/2oz/½ cup flaked (sliced) almonds

juice of ½ lemon

lemon wedges, to serve

1 Wash the fish, dry with kitchen paper and coat them with seasoned flour, shaking off any excess.

2 Heat half the butter with the oil in a large frying pan. When the mixture begins to foam, add one or two fish.

3 Cook over medium heat for 3–5 minutes on each side or until golden brown and cooked through. Lift out, drain on kitchen paper and keep warm.

4 Cook the remaining fish, then wipe the pan out with kitchen paper. Add the remaining butter and when foaming add the almonds. Cook gently, stirring frequently, until the almonds are golden brown. Remove from the heat and add the lemon juice.

5 Sprinkle the almonds and pan juices over the trout and serve immediately with lemon wedges for squeezing over.

Cook's tip When buying the trout, choose a size that will fit inside your frying pan.

Variation The trout can be grilled (broiled) if preferred. Omit the flour coating. Melt half the butter and brush over both sides of the fish. Put the fish under a medium-hot grill (broiler) and cook for 5–7 minutes on each side until golden brown and cooked all the way through. Cook the almonds in butter as in step 4 above.

Energy 475kcal/1978kJ; Protein 39.2g; Carbohydrate 7.6g, of which sugars 0.8g; Fat 32.2g, of which saturates 12.4g; Cholesterol 187mg; Calcium 101mg; Fibre 1.2g; Sodium 249mg

Fish and chips

Here is one of England's national dishes. Use white fish of your choice – cod, haddock, hake, huss, plaice, skate or whiting – and cook in batches so that each piece of fish and all the chips are perfectly crisp. Salt and vinegar are the traditional accompaniments.

Serves 4

115g/4oz/1 cup self-raising (self-rising) flour

150ml/¼ pint/⅔ cup water

675g/1½lb potatoes

oil, for deep frying

675g/1½lb skinned cod fillet, cut into four pieces

salt and pepper

lemon wedges, to serve

1 Stir the flour and salt together in a bowl, then make a well in the centre. Gradually whisk in the water to make a smooth batter. Leave for 30 minutes.

2 Using a sharp knife, cut the potatoes into strips about 1cm/½in wide and 5cm/2in long. Put the potatoes in a colander and rinse them with cold water, then drain and dry well.

3 Heat the oil in a deep-fat fryer or large heavy pan to 150°C/300°F. Using a wire basket, lower the potatoes in batches into the hot oil and cook for 5–6 minutes, shaking the basket occasionally until the chips are soft but not browned. Remove the chips from the oil and drain them thoroughly on kitchen paper.

4 Increase the heat of the oil in the fryer to 190°C/375°F. Season the pieces of fish with salt and pepper. Stir the batter, then dip the fish into it, one piece at a time, allowing the excess to drain off.

5 Working in two batches if necessary, lower the fish into the hot oil and fry for 6–8 minutes, until crisp and brown. Drain the fish on kitchen paper and keep warm.

6 Make sure the oil is hot again then add a batch of chips, cooking for 2–3 minutes, until brown and crisp. Keep hot while cooking the other batches. Sprinkle with salt and serve with the fish, accompanied by lemon wedges.

Energy 521kcal/2188kJ; Protein 36.3g; Carbohydrate 48.9g, of which sugars 2.6g; Fat 21.3g, of which saturates 2.7g; Cholesterol 78mg; Calcium 126mg; Fibre 2.6g; Sodium 223mg

Haddock in cheese sauce

A relative of cod, haddock is one of the nation's preferred white fish, though unfortunately North Sea supplies have declined considerably in recent years. Other white fish can be used in place of haddock in this flavourful dish – try hake, coley or whiting.

Serves 4

1kg/2¼lb haddock fillets

300ml/½ pint/1¼ cups milk

1 small onion, thinly sliced

2 bay leaves

a few black peppercorns

25g/1oz/2 tbsp butter

25g/1oz/2 tbsp flour

5ml/1 tsp English (hot) mustard

115g/4oz mature hard cheese such as Cheddar, grated

salt and ground black pepper

1 Put the fish in a pan large enough to hold it in a single layer. Add the milk, onion, bay leaves and peppercorns and heat slowly until small bubbles are rising to the surface.

2 Cover and simmer very gently for 5–8 minutes, until the fish is just cooked. Lift out with a slotted spoon, straining and reserving the cooking liquid. Flake the fish, removing any bones.

Variation This dish can be made with smoked haddock, use fillets that have been mildly smoked. You can also use half smoked and half unsmoked.

3 To make the sauce, melt the butter in a saucepan, stir in the flour and cook gently, stirring all the time, for about 1 minute (do not allow it to brown). Remove from the heat and gradually stir in the strained milk. Return the pan to the heat and cook, stirring, until the mixture thickens and comes to the boil. Stir in the mustard and three-quarters of the cheese and season to taste.

4 Gently stir the fish into the sauce and spoon the mixture into individual flameproof dishes. Sprinkle the remaining cheese over the top. Put under a hot grill (broiler) until bubbling and golden. Serve with crusty bread.

Cook's tip.The fish can be left whole if you prefer, spoon the sauce over them before grilling.

Energy 430kcal/1809kJ; Protein 58.2g; Carbohydrate 9.6g, of which sugars 4.5g; Fat 17.4g, of which saturates 10.6g; Cholesterol 136mg; Calcium 351mg; Fibre 0.4g; Sodium 446mg

Seafood pancakes

English pancakes can be traced back as far as the 15th century, when the batter would have been made with eggs, flour and water. Three hundred years later, the water was replaced with beer or ale and later still with milk.

Serves 4

For the pancakes

115g/4oz/1 cup plain (all-purpose) flour

pinch of salt

1 egg

300ml/½ pint/1¼ cups milk

15ml/1 tbsp melted butter

oil or melted butter, for cooking

For the filling

300ml/½ pint/1¼ cups milk

150ml/¼ pint/⅔ cup fish stock

25g/1oz/2 tbsp flour

25g/1oz/2 tbsp butter

350g/12oz skinless fish fillets, such as haddock and salmon, cut into bite size pieces

115g/4oz peeled prawns (shrimp)

large handful of baby spinach leaves

50g/2oz cheese, such as Cheddar or Lancashire, grated

1 To make the pancakes, sift the flour and salt into a bowl and break the egg into it. Gradually beat in the milk to make a smooth batter and then stir in 15ml/1 tbsp melted butter.

2 Put a 20cm/8in non-stick frying pan over a medium heat and brush with oil or butter. When hot, add 45ml/3 tbsp batter, tilting to cover the surface. Cook until the underside is golden brown then flip over and briefly cook the other side. Repeat with the remaining batter to make eight pancakes. Keep warm.

3 To make the filling, put the milk, stock, flour and butter into a pan. Bring to the boil, whisking continuously, until the sauce thickens. Add the fish pieces and simmer gently for 3–4 minutes or until the fish is just cooked. Stir in the prawns and spinach.

4 Cook until the prawns are heated through and the spinach is wilted. Stir in the cheese. Remove from the heat.

5 Spoon the fish mixture into the centre of the pancakes and roll up or fold into triangles. Serve immediately.

Energy 393kcal/1647kJ; Protein 26.7g; Carbohydrate 25.4g, of which sugars 5.7g; Fat 21.2g, of which saturates 11.9g; Cholesterol 203mg; Calcium 273mg; Fibre 0.8g; Sodium 513mg

Smoked fish soufflé

The fluffy savoury soufflé comes from French cuisine, but was made in grand English kitchens by 19th-century chefs such as Antonin Carême, who cooked for the Prince Regent. Serve it puffed up and straight out of the oven, before it has time to settle and fall.

Serves 4

225g/8oz skinless smoked haddock

300ml/½ pint/1¼ cups milk

2 bay leaves (optional)

40g/1½oz/3 tbsp butter, plus extra for greasing

40g/1½oz/5 tbsp plain (all-purpose) flour

55g/2oz mature Cheddar cheese

5ml/1 tsp English (hot) mustard

4 egg yolks

5 egg whites

ground black pepper

1 Put the fish into a pan just large enough to hold it in a single layer, and add the milk and bay leaves (if using). Heat slowly until the milk is very hot, with small bubbles rising to the surface, but not boiling. Cover and simmer very gently for 5–8 minutes until the fish is just cooked.

2 Lift out the fish with a slotted spoon, reserving the cooking liquid, and remove any bones. Discard the bay leaves and break the fish into flakes. Preheat the oven to 190°C/375°F/Gas 5 and butter a 20cm/8in soufflé dish.

3 Melt the butter in a pan, stir in the flour and cook gently for 1 minute, stirring. Remove from the heat and gradually stir in the reserved cooking liquid. Cook, stirring constantly until the sauce thickens and comes to the boil.

4 Remove from the heat. Stir in the cheese, mustard, pepper and fish.

5 Beat in the egg yolks, one at a time. Whisk the egg whites until stiff. Stir a little egg white into the sauce then use a large metal spoon to fold in the rest.

6 Pour the mixture into the prepared dish and cook in the hot oven for about 40 minutes until risen and just firm to the touch. Serve immediately.

Energy 325kcal/1356kJ; Protein 24.4g; Carbohydrate 11.4g, of which sugars 3.8g; Fat 20.3g, of which saturates 10.7g; Cholesterol 272mg; Calcium 247mg; Fibre 0.3g; Sodium 706mg

Fisherman's casserole

The English have been known to limit their choice to just a few well-loved species of fish such as cod and herring. Today, as stocks dwindle, fish-eaters are becoming much more open-minded and appreciative of the wide variety of fish caught around English shores.

Serves 4

500g/1¼lb mixed fish fillets, such as haddock, bass, red mullet, salmon

500g/1¼lb mixed shellfish, such as squid strips, mussels, cockles and prawns (shrimp)

15ml/1 tbsp oil

25g/1oz/2 tbsp butter

1 medium onion, finely chopped

1 carrot, finely chopped

3 celery sticks, finely chopped

30ml/2 tbsp plain (all-purpose) flour

600ml/1 pint/2½ cups fish stock

300ml/½pt/1¼ cups dry (hard) cider

350g/12oz small new potatoes, halved

150m/¼ pint/⅔ cup double (heavy) cream

small handful of chopped mixed herbs such as parsley, chives and dill

salt and ground black pepper

1 Wash the fish fillets and dry on kitchen paper. With a sharp knife, remove the skin, feel carefully for any bones and extract them. Cut the fish into large, even chunks.

2 Prepare the shellfish, shelling the prawns if necessary. Scrub the mussels and cockles, discarding any with broken shells or that do not close when given a sharp tap. Pull off the black tufts (beards) attached to the mussels.

3 Heat the oil and butter in a large saucepan, add the onion, carrot and celery and cook over a medium heat, stirring occasionally, until beginning to soften and turn golden brown. Add the flour, and cook for 1 minute.

4 Remove the pan from the heat and gradually stir in the fish stock and cider. Return the pan to the heat and cook, stirring continuously, until the mixture comes to the boil and thickens.

Cook's tip This simple recipe can be adapted according to the varieties of fish and shellfish that are obtainable on the day – it is delicious whatever mixture you choose.

5 Add the potatoes. Bring the sauce back to the boil, then cover and simmer gently for 10–15 minutes until the potatoes are nearly tender.

6 Add all the fish and shellfish and stir in gently.

7 Stir in the cream. Bring back to a gentle simmer, then cover the pan and cook gently for 5–10 minutes or until the pieces of fish are cooked through and all the shells have opened. Adjust the seasoning to taste and gently stir in the herbs. Serve immediately.

Energy 583kcal/2439kJ; Protein 49.3g; Carbohydrate 25.3g, of which sugars 6.1g; Fat 30.2g, of which saturates 16.5g; Cholesterol 354mg; Calcium 199mg; Fibre 2.5g; Sodium 404mg

Meat Dishes

England takes great pride in its Sunday roast – a succulent joint of beef, lamb or pork cooked to perfection in the oven and served with all the trimmings. Then there are pot roasts, stews and braises, and comforting puddings and pies, not to mention bacon, chops and steaks and a wonderful variety of sausages to grill, pan-fry or bake.

Rib of beef with Yorkshire puddings

Mention English food and most people think of this quintessential dish, which is traditionally served for Sunday lunch and on special occasions. In Victorian days in the north-east of England, roast beef would have been traditional fare on Christmas day. The accompanying batter pudding was not served alongside it until well into the 18th century and in Yorkshire it is still sometimes eaten with gravy before the meat course.

Serves 6–8

rib of beef joint, weighing about 3kg/6½lb

oil, for brushing

salt and ground black pepper

For the Yorkshire puddings

115g/4oz/1 cup plain (all-purpose) flour

1.5ml/¼ tsp salt

1 egg

200ml/7fl oz/scant 1 cup milk

oil or beef dripping, for greasing

For the horseradish cream

60–75ml/4–5 tbsp finely grated fresh horseradish

300ml/½ pint/1¼ cups soured cream

30ml/2 tbsp cider vinegar or white wine vinegar

10ml/2 tsp caster (superfine) sugar

For the gravy

600ml/1 pint/2½ cups good beef stock

1 Preheat the oven to 220°C/425°F/Gas 7. Weigh the joint and calculate the cooking time required as follows: 10–15 minutes per 500g/1¼lb for rare beef, 15–20 minutes for medium and 20–25 minutes for well done.

Cook's tip To avoid the pungent smell (and tears) produced by grating horseradish, use a jar of preserved grated horseradish.

2 Put the joint into a large roasting pan. Brush it all over with oil and season with salt and pepper. Put into the hot oven and cook for 30 minutes, until the beef is browned. Lower the oven temperature to 160°C/325°F/Gas 3 and cook for the calculated time, spooning the juices over the meat occasionally during cooking.

3 For the Yorkshire pudding, sift the flour and salt into a bowl and break the egg into it. Make the milk up to 300ml/½ pint/1¼ cups with water and gradually whisk into the flour to make a smooth batter. Leave to stand while the beef cooks. Generously grease eight Yorkshire pudding tins (muffin pans) measuring about 10cm/4in.

4 For the horseradish cream, put all the ingredients into a bowl and mix well. Cover and chill until required.

5 At the end of its cooking time, remove the beef from the oven, cover with foil and leave to stand for 30–40 minutes while you cook the Yorkshire puddings and make the gravy.

6 Increase the oven temperature to 220°C/425°F/Gas 7 and put the prepared tins on the top shelf for 5 minutes until very hot. Pour in the batter and cook for about 15 minutes until well risen, crisp and golden brown.

7 To make the gravy, transfer the beef to a warmed serving plate. Pour off the fat from the roasting pan, leaving the meat juices. Add the stock to the pan, bring to the boil and bubble until reduced by about half. Season to taste.

8 Carve the beef and serve with the gravy, Yorkshire puddings, roast potatoes and horseradish cream.

Energy 1037kcal/4338kJ; Protein 129g; Carbohydrate 15.1g, of which sugars 4.1g; Fat 51.5g, of which saturates 24.3g; Cholesterol 352mg; Calcium 123mg; Fibre 0.5g; Sodium 249mg

Pot-roasted beef with stout

This method is ideal for cuts that need tenderizing by long, slow cooking. Boned and rolled joints such as brisket, silverside and topside of beef, which are full of flavour, are perfect.

Serves 6

30ml/2 tbsp vegetable oil

900g/2lb rolled brisket of beef

2 medium onions, roughly chopped

2 celery sticks, thickly sliced

450g/1lb carrots, cut into large chunks

675g/1½lb potatoes, peeled and cut into large chunks

30ml/2 tbsp plain (all-purpose) flour

450ml/¾ pint/ 2 cups beef stock

300ml/½ pint/1¼ cups stout

1 bay leaf

45ml/3 tbsp chopped fresh thyme

5ml/1 tsp soft light brown sugar

30ml/2 tbsp wholegrain mustard

15ml/1 tbsp tomato purée (paste)

salt and ground black pepper

1 Preheat the oven to 180°C/350°F/ Gas 4. Heat the oil in a large flameproof casserole and brown the beef until golden brown all over.

2 Lift the beef from the pan and drain on kitchen paper. Add the onions to the pan and cook for about 4 minutes, until just beginning to soften and brown.

3 Add the celery, carrots and potatoes to the casserole and cook over a medium heat for 2–3 minutes, or until they are just beginning to colour.

4 Add the flour and cook for a further 1 minute, stirring continuously. Gradually pour in the beef stock and the stout. Heat until the mixture comes to the boil, stirring frequently.

5 Stir in the bay leaf, thyme, sugar, mustard, tomato purée and seasoning. Place the meat on top, cover tightly and transfer the casserole to the hot oven.

6 Cook for about 2½ hours, or until the tender. Adjust the seasoning, to taste. To serve, carve the beef into thick slices and serve with the vegetables and plenty of gravy.

Energy 415kcal/1743kJ; Protein 36g; Carbohydrate 35.6g, of which sugars 13.1g; Fat 14g, of which saturates 4.4g; Cholesterol 81mg; Calcium 66mg; Fibre 4.2g; Sodium 284mg

Braised beef with herb dumplings

Dumplings, probably originally made from bread dough, have been added to English stews for centuries to satisfy hearty appetites, and are particularly associated with Norfolk.

Serves 4

25g/1oz/2 tbsp butter

30ml/2 tbsp oil

115g/4oz/⅔ cup streaky (fatty) bacon, chopped

900g/2lb lean braising steak, cut into chunks

45ml/3 tbsp plain (all-purpose) flour

450ml/¾ pint/scant 2 cups beer

450ml/¾ pint/scant 2 cups beef stock

1 bouquet garni

8 shallots

175g/6oz/2 cups small mushrooms

salt and ground black pepper

For the herb dumplings

115g/4oz/1 cup self-raising (self-rising) flour

50g/2oz/scant ½ cup shredded suet

2.5ml/½ tsp salt

2.5ml/½ tsp mustard powder

15ml/1 tbsp chopped fresh parsley

15ml/1 tbsp fresh thyme leaves

1 In a large frying pan, melt half the butter with half the oil, add the bacon and brown. Transfer to a casserole.

2 Brown the beef quickly in the frying pan in batches, then transfer it to the casserole using a slotted spoon.

3 Stir the flour into the fat in the pan. Add the beer, stock and seasoning and bring to the boil, stirring constantly. Pour over the meat, add the bouquet garni, cover and place in a cold oven set to 200°C/400°F/Gas 6. Cook for 30 minutes then reduce the temperature to 160°C/325°F/Gas 3 and cook for 1 hour.

4 Heat the remaining butter and oil in a frying pan and cook the shallots until golden. Lift out and set aside. Add the mushrooms and cook quickly for 2–3 minutes. Stir the vegetables into the stew, cover and cook for 30 minutes.

5 In a bowl, mix together the dumpling ingredients. Add cold water to make a soft, sticky dough. Roll into 12 balls and place on top of the stew. Cover, cook for a further 25 minutes, and serve.

Energy 754kcal/3148kJ; Protein 60.8g; Carbohydrate 36.6g, of which sugars 3.8g; Fat 41.4g, of which saturates 14.9g; Cholesterol 163mg; Calcium 147mg; Fibre 2.1g; Sodium 700mg

Steak and kidney pudding

This classic dish is in fact a 19th-century invention that has, in a relatively short time, become one of England's most famous dishes. In Victorian days it would also have included oysters, then incredibly cheap, and some versions also contain mushrooms.

Serves 6

500g/1¼lb lean stewing steak, cut into cubes

225g/8oz beef kidney or lamb's kidneys, skin and core removed and cut into small cubes

1 medium onion, finely chopped

30ml/2 tbsp finely chopped fresh herbs, such as parsley and thyme

30ml/2 tbsp plain (all-purpose) flour

275g/10oz/2½ cups self-raising (self-rising) flour

150g/5oz/1 cup shredded suet

finely grated rind of 1 small lemon

about 120ml/4fl oz/½ cup beef stock or water

salt and ground black pepper

1 Put the stewing steak into a large mixing bowl and add the kidneys, onion and chopped herbs. Sprinkle the plain flour and seasoning over the top and mix well.

2 To make the pastry, sift the self-raising flour into another large bowl. Stir in the suet and lemon rind. Add sufficient cold water to bind the ingredients and gather into a soft dough.

3 On a lightly floured surface knead the dough gently, and then roll out to make a circle measuring about 35cm/14in across. Cut out one-quarter of the circle, roll up and put aside.

4 Lightly butter a 1.75 litre/3 pint heatproof bowl. Line the bowl with the rolled out dough, pressing the cut edges together and allowing the pastry to overlap the top of the bowl slightly.

5 Spoon the steak mixture into the lined bowl, packing it in carefully, so as not to split the pastry.

6 Pour in sufficient stock to reach no more than three-quarters of the way up the filling. (Any stock remaining can be heated and poured into the cooked pudding to thin the gravy if desired.)

7 Roll out the reserved pastry into a circle to form a lid and lay it over the filling, pinching the edges together to seal them well.

8 Cover with greaseproof paper or baking parchment, pleated in the centre to allow the pudding to rise, and then with a large sheet of foil (again pleated at the centre). Tuck the edges under and press them tightly to the sides of the basin until securely sealed (alternatively, tie with string). Steam for about 5 hours.

9 Carefully remove the foil and paper, slide a knife around the sides of the pudding and turn out on to a warmed serving plate.

Energy 436kcal/1835kJ; Protein 31.1g; Carbohydrate 49.5g, of which sugars 4.8g; Fat 13.9g, of which saturates 3.6g; Cholesterol 166mg; Calcium 201mg; Fibre 1.9g; Sodium 380mg

Roast pork with crackling and apple sauce

A roast joint makes a traditional centrepiece for Sunday lunch with family or friends. Since Roman times it has been customary to offset the richness of the pork with sharp fruit flavours. Serve this fruit-stuffed loin of pork with freshly cooked seasonal vegetables.

Serves 6

15ml/1 tbsp light olive oil

2 leeks, chopped

150g/5oz/⅔ cup ready-to-eat dried apricots, chopped

150g/5oz/1 cup dried dates, stoned (pitted) and chopped

75g/3oz/1½ cups fresh white breadcrumbs

2 eggs, beaten

15ml/1 tbsp fresh thyme leaves

1.5kg/3¼lb boned loin of pork

salt and ground black pepper

For the apple sauce

450g/1lb cooking apples

30ml/2 tbsp cider or water

25g/1oz/2 tbsp butter

about 25g/1oz/2 tbsp caster (superfine) sugar

1 Preheat the oven to 220°C/425°F/Gas 7. To make the stuffing, heat the oil in a large pan and cook the leeks until softened. Remove from the heat and stir in the apricots, dates, breadcrumbs, eggs and thyme and season with salt and pepper.

2 Lay the pork skin side up, and use a very sharp knife to score the rind into diamonds. (You may find it easier to do this with a clean craft knife or scalpel.)

3 Turn the joint over and cut vertically down the centre of the meat to within 1cm/½in of the rind and fat, then cut horizontally from the middle outwards towards each side to open out the joint for stuffing.

4 Spoon half the stuffing into the cut surfaces, then fold the meat over. Tie the joint back into its original shape, then place in a roasting pan and rub the skin liberally with salt.

5 Put the joint into the hot oven and cook for 40 minutes. Reduce the temperature to 190°C/375°F/Gas 5 and cook for a further 1½ hours, or until the meat is cooked through – the juices should run clear when the meat is pierced with a sharp knife.

6 Meanwhile, shape the remaining stuffing into walnut-sized balls. Arrange on a tray, cover with clear film (plastic wrap) and chill until 30 minutes before the pork is cooked. Then add the balls to the roasting pan and baste them with the cooking juices from the meat.

7 To make the apple sauce, peel, core and chop the apples, then place in a small pan with the cider or water and cook, stirring occasionally, for 5–10 minutes, or until very soft. Beat well or blend in a blender or food processor until smooth. Beat in the butter and sugar to taste. Reheat the apple sauce just before serving, if necessary.

8 When the meat is cooked, cover it closely with foil and leave to stand in a warm place for 10 minutes to rest before carving. Carve the pork into thick slices and serve with pieces of the crackling, the stuffing balls and the apple sauce.

Energy 582kcal/2452kJ; Protein 59.9g; Carbohydrate 48.3g, of which sugars 38.6g; Fat 17.9g, of which saturates 6.5g; Cholesterol 230mg; Calcium 91mg; Fibre 5.2g; Sodium 327mg

Toad in the hole

Early versions of toad in the hole, in the 18th century, were made with pieces of meat rather than sausages: one very grand recipe even called for fillet steak. Today the "toads" are sausages and the batter is that used for Yorkshire pudding. There is an English pub game of the same name, where discs are thrown at a hole in the table.

Serves 6

175g/6oz/1½ cups plain (all-purpose) flour

2.5ml/½ tsp salt

2 eggs

300ml/½ pint/1¼ cups milk

30ml/2 tbsp oil

500g/1¼lb meaty butcher's sausages

3 Pour the oil into a roasting pan and add the sausages (cut in half crosswise if large). Put into the hot oven and cook for about 10 minutes until the oil is very hot and the sausages begin to brown.

4 Stir the batter and quickly pour it around the sausages and return to the oven. Cook for about 45 minutes or until the batter is puffed up, set and golden brown. Serve immediately.

1 Preheat the oven to 220°C/425°F/ Gas 7. To make the batter, sift the flour and salt into a bowl, make a well in the centre and break the eggs into it.

2 Mix the milk with 300ml/½ pint/ 1¼ cups cold water. Using a whisk, gradually stir the milk mixture into the bowl with the eggs, incorporating the flour and beating well to make a smooth batter. Leave to stand.

Energy 497kcal/2070kJ; Protein 14.5g; Carbohydrate 32.1g, of which sugars 3.8g; Fat 35.4g, of which saturates 13.6g; Cholesterol 109mg; Calcium 141mg; Fibre 1.3g; Sodium 616mg

Rissoles

In a 16th-century English recipe for "rissheshewes", finely chopped cooked meat was mixed with breadcrumbs and bound into little cakes with beaten eggs and a thick gravy. These contemporary rissoles have been adapted to feature mashed potato as well as breadcrumbs, which makes the mixture easier to shape and coat with crumbs.

Serves 4

675g/1½lb potatoes, peeled

350g/12oz cooked beef or lamb, such as the remains of a joint, trimmed of excess fat

1 small onion

5ml/1 tsp Worcestershire sauce

30ml/2 tbsp chopped fresh herbs, such as parsley, mint and chives

30ml/2 tbsp plain (all-purpose) flour

2 eggs, beaten

115g/4oz/2 cups fresh breadcrumbs

oil for frying

salt and ground black pepper

brown sauce, to serve

1 Cook the whole potatoes in boiling water for about 20 minutes or until completely soft. Meanwhile, mince (grind) or chop the meat very finely. Finely chop the onion.

2 Drain the potatoes and mash them thoroughly by pushing the warm potatoes through a ricer, passing them through a mouli, or mashing them with a potato masher or fork.

3 In a large mixing bowl combine the meat and onion with the potatoes, Worcestershire sauce, herbs and seasoning, beating well. Shape the mixture into eight patties or sausages.

Cook's tip Chilling the potato and meat mixture before shaping the rissoles will make it easier to handle.

4 Dip in the flour, then in the beaten egg and finally in the breadcrumbs, gently shaking off any excess.

5 Heat enough oil to cover the base of a large frying pan and cook the rissoles over a medium heat, turning once or twice, until crisp and golden brown. Drain and serve with brown sauce.

Energy 519kcal/2184kJ; Protein 27.4g; Carbohydrate 56.7g, of which sugars 4.1g; Fat 22g, of which saturates 6.5g; Cholesterol 162mg; Calcium 86mg; Fibre 2.8g; Sodium 363mg

Braised sausages with onions, celeriac and apple

England boasts a wealth of wonderful sausages made by artisan producers across the regions. For this recipe, choose your favourite good-quality sausages, such as traditional pork, Cumberland, or something more unusual, such as duck, venison or wild boar.

Serves 4

30ml/2 tbsp oil

8 meaty sausages

2 onions, sliced

15ml/1 tbsp plain (all-purpose) flour

400ml/14fl oz/1⅔ cups dry (hard) cider

350g/12oz celeriac, cut into chunks

15ml/1 tbsp Worcestershire sauce

15ml/1 tbsp chopped fresh sage

2 small cooking apples

salt and ground black pepper

1 Preheat the oven to 180°C/350°F/ Gas 4. Heat the oil in a frying pan, add the sausages and fry for about 5 minutes until evenly browned.

2 Transfer the sausages to an ovenproof cassserole dish and drain any excess oil from the pan to leave 15ml/1 tbsp. Add the onions and cook for a few minutes, stirring occasionally, until softened and turning golden.

3 Stir in the flour, then gradually add the cider and bring to the boil, stirring. Add the celeriac and stir in the Worcestershire sauce and sage. Season with salt and black pepper.

4 Pour the cider and celeriac mixture over the sausages. Cover, put into the hot oven and cook for 30 minutes, or until the celeriac is soft.

5 Quarter the apples, remove their cores and cut into thick slices. Stir the apple slices into the casserole, cover and cook for a further 10–15 minutes, or until the apples are just tender. Taste and adjust the seasoning if necessary before serving.

Energy 508kcal/2114kJ; Protein 12.7g; Carbohydrate 29.3g, of which sugars 13.6g; Fat 35.8g, of which saturates 12.3g; Cholesterol 45mg; Calcium 131mg; Fibre 3.3g; Sodium 1019mg

Liver and bacon casserole

Instead of the long, slow cooking of a traditional casserole, this dish of lamb's liver and bacon is cooked in less than half an hour. You could, of course, cook calf's or pig's liver in the same way. Baby potatoes and green beans make ideal accompaniments.

Serves 4

30ml/2 tbsp olive oil

225g/8oz rindless unsmoked lean bacon rashers (strips), cut into pieces

2 onions, halved and sliced

175g/6oz/2 cups mushrooms, halved

450g/1lb lamb's liver, sliced

25g/1oz/2 tbsp butter

15ml/1 tbsp soy sauce

30ml/2 tbsp plain (all-purpose) flour

150ml/¼ pint/⅔ cup hot, well-flavoured chicken stock

salt and ground black pepper

1 Heat the oil in a frying pan, add the bacon and fry until crisp.

2 Add the sliced onions and cook for about 10 minutes, stirring frequently, until softened and turning golden. Add the mushrooms to the pan and cook for a further 1 minute.

3 Using a slotted spoon, remove the bacon and vegetables from the pan and keep warm.

4 Add the liver to the fat remaining in the pan and cook over a high heat for 3–4 minutes, turning once, until browned on both sides. Remove the liver from the pan and keep warm.

5 Melt the butter in the pan, add the soy sauce and flour and blend together. Gradually stir in the stock and bring to the boil, stirring until thickened. Return the liver, bacon and vegetables to the pan and stir into the gravy. Heat through for 1 minute, season to taste and serve immediately.

Energy 431kcal/1796kJ; Protein 34.7g; Carbohydrate 12.3g, of which sugars 6.1g; Fat 27.4g, of which saturates 9.4g; Cholesterol 527mg; Calcium 46mg; Fibre 2g; Sodium 1259mg

Somerset cider-glazed ham

William the Conqueror is credited with bringing the art of cider-making to England from Normandy in 1066. This wonderful West Country ham glazed with cider is traditionally served with cranberry sauce and is ideal for Christmas or Boxing Day.

Serves 8–10

2kg/4½lb middle gammon (smoked or cured ham) joint

2 small onions

about 30 whole cloves

3 bay leaves

10 black peppercorns

1.3 litres/2¼ pints/5⅔ cups medium-dry (hard) cider

45ml/3 tbsp soft light brown sugar

For the cranberry sauce

350g/12oz/3 cups cranberries

175g/6oz/¾ cup light brown sugar

grated rind and juice of 2 clementines

30ml/2 tbsp port

1 Weigh the ham and calculate the cooking time at 20 minutes per 450g/1lb, then place it in a large pan. Stud the onions with 5–10 cloves and add to the pan together with the bay leaves and peppercorns.

2 Add 1.2 litres/2 pints/5 cups of the cider and enough water just to cover the ham. Heat until simmering and skim off the scum that rises to the surface.

3 Start timing the cooking from the moment the stock begins to simmer. Cover with a lid or foil and simmer gently for the calculated time. Towards the end of the cooking time, preheat the oven to 220°C/425°F/Gas 7.

4 Lift the ham out of the pan. Leave to stand until cool enough to handle.

5 Heat the sugar and remaining cider in a pan until the sugar dissolves. Bubble gently for about 5 minutes to make a dark glaze. Remove the pan from the heat and leave to cool for 5 minutes.

6 Carefully and evenly, cut off the rind of the ham, then score the fat to make a neat diamond pattern. Place the ham in a roasting tin. Press a clove into the centre of each diamond, then carefully spoon the glaze over. Put into the hot oven and cook for 20–25 minutes, or until brown, glistening and crisp.

7 To make the cranberry sauce, simmer all the ingredients in a heavy pan for 15–20 minutes, stirring frequently, until the fruit bursts and the sauce thickens. Pour into a serving dish.

8 Serve the ham hot or cold with the cranberry sauce.

Cook's tips If the ham is likely to be very salty, soak it overnight in cold water to remove excess salt before cooking. Your butcher will advise you.
• Reserve the stock used to cook the ham and use it to make a hearty split pea or lentil soup.

Energy 368kcal/1541kJ; Protein 39.6g; Carbohydrate 15.2g, of which sugars 15.2g; Fat 16.9g, of which saturates 5.6g; Cholesterol 52mg; Calcium 25mg; Fibre 0.6g; Sodium 1982mg

Poultry and Game

Most English households used to keep poultry, if only
a few hens, to provide them with eggs, but in small
holdings and farms ducks, turkeys and geese would
also be kept as a source of meat for the table.
Seasonal game from England's woods and moors has
always been popular too with birds, venison, rabbits
and hares all supplying sustenance at times when
farmed meat was expensive.

Stuffed roast chicken with bread sauce

Chicken today is a popular choice for roasting and is plentiful and cheap. However, free-range and organic birds taste best and are more like the birds that previous generations regarded as a luxury food. Roast sausages and potatoes with the bird for a complete meal.

Serves 6

1 chicken weighing about 1.8kg/4lb, with giblets and neck if possible

1 small onion, sliced

1 small carrot, sliced

small bunch of parsley and thyme

15g/½oz/1 tbsp butter

30ml/2 tbsp oil

6 rashers (strips) fatty bacon

15ml/1 tbsp plain (all-purpose) flour

300ml/½ pint/1¼ cups chicken stock

salt and ground black pepper

For the stuffing

1 onion, finely chopped

50g/2oz/4 tbsp butter

150g/5oz/2½ cups fresh white breadcrumbs

15ml/1 tbsp chopped fresh parsley

15ml/1 tbsp chopped fresh herbs, such as thyme, marjoram and chives

grated rind and juice of ½ lemon

For the bread sauce

1 small onion, sliced

1 bay leaf

6 black peppercorns

2 whole cloves

pinch of mace or grated nutmeg

400ml/14fl oz/1⅔ cups milk

50g/2oz/1 cup fresh breadcrumbs

25g/1oz/2 tbsp butter.

1 Put the giblets and neck into a pan with the sliced onion and carrot and the bunch of parsley and thyme. Season with salt and pepper. Cover generously with cold water, bring to the boil and simmer gently for about 1 hour. Strain the stock, discarding the giblets. Preheat the oven to 200°C/400°F/Gas 6.

2 To make the stuffing, cook the onion in the butter in a large pan over low heat until soft. Remove from the heat and stir in the breadcrumbs, herbs, lemon rind and juice, salt and pepper.

3 Spoon the stuffing into the neck cavity of the chicken and secure the opening with a small skewer. Weigh the stuffed chicken and calculate the cooking time at 20 minutes per 450g/1lb plus 20 minutes extra. Spread the chicken breast with the butter, then put the oil into a roasting pan and sit the bird in it. Season and lay the bacon rashers over the breast.

4 Put the chicken into the hot oven. After 20 minutes, reduce the temperature to 180°C/350°F/Gas 4 and cook for the remaining time. To check the chicken is cooked, insert a sharp knife between the body and the thigh: if the juices run clear with no hint of blood, it is done.

5 Meanwhile, make the bread sauce. Into a pan, put the onion, bay leaf, peppercorns, cloves, mace and milk. Bring slowly to the boil, remove from the heat, cover and leave to stand for 30 minutes or longer to infuse. Strain and return the milk to the cleaned pan, add the breadcrumbs and seasoning. Heat until bubbling and simmer gently for about 10 minutes until thick and creamy. Stir in the butter and it is ready to serve.

6 Transfer the cooked chicken to a serving dish and allow it to rest for 10 minutes in a warm place while you make the gravy.

7 To make the gravy, pour off the excess fat from the roasting pan, then sprinkle in the flour. Cook gently, stirring, for 1–2 minutes. Gradually add the stock, scraping the pan to lift the residue and stirring well until smooth. Bring to the boil, stirring and adding extra stock if necessary. Adjust the seasoning to taste.

8 Carve the chicken, and serve with the gravy and bread sauce.

Cook's tip If you prefer not to stuff the chicken, the stuffing can be formed into small balls and baked around the bird for the last 20–30 minutes of the cooking time.

Energy 823kcal/3420kJ; Protein 55.7g; Carbohydrate 21.1g, of which sugars 19.1g; Fat 57.8g, of which saturates 19.7g; Cholesterol 383mg; Calcium 113mg; Fibre 4.9g; Sodium 252mg

Coronation chicken

Originally devised as part of the feast to celebrate the coronation of Elizabeth II in 1953, this chicken salad has been appearing on buffet tables countrywide ever since.

Serves 8

½ lemon

2.25kg/5lb chicken

1 onion, quartered

1 carrot, quartered

1 large bouquet garni

8 black peppercorns, crushed

salt

watercress sprigs, to garnish

For the sauce

1 small onion, chopped

15g/½oz/1 tbsp butter

15ml/1 tbsp curry paste

15ml/1 tbsp tomato purée (paste)

125ml/4fl oz/½ cup red wine

1 bay leaf

juice of ½ lemon, or to taste

10–15ml/2–3 tsp apricot jam

300ml/½ pint/1¼ cups mayonnaise

125ml/4fl oz/½ cup whipping cream

salt and ground black pepper

1 Put the lemon half in the chicken cavity, then place it in a close-fitting pan. Add the vegetables, bouquet garni, peppercorns and a little salt.

2 Add water to come two-thirds of the way up the chicken, bring just to the boil, cover and cook very gently for 1½ hours, until the chicken juices run clear. Leave to cool. When the chicken is cold remove all the skin and bones and chop the flesh.

Cook's tips A few walnut pieces or slices of celery would add some crunch and texture to the dish.

3 To make the sauce, cook the onion in the butter until soft. Add the curry paste, tomato purée, wine, bay leaf and lemon juice, then cook gently for 10 minutes. Add the jam, press through a sieve (strainer) and cool.

4 Beat the sauce into the mayonnaise. Whip the cream and fold it in; add seasoning and lemon juice, then stir in the chicken. Garnish and serve.

Energy 587kcal/2429kJ; Protein 10.1g; Carbohydrate 17.1g, of which sugars 4.7g; Fat 51.6g, of which saturates 8.8g; Cholesterol 228mg; Calcium 97mg; Fibre 1.1g; Sodium 401mg

Devilled chicken

Applying hot or spicy seasonings to food before cooking, known as devilling, became very popular in the 1800s, and was used to revive cold, cooked meat for serving the next day.

Serves 4–6

6 chicken drumsticks

6 chicken thighs

15ml/1 tbsp oil

45ml/3 tbsp chutney, finely chopped

15ml/1 tbsp Worcestershire sauce

10ml/2 tsp English (hot) mustard

1.5ml/¼ tsp cayenne pepper

1.5ml/¼ tsp ground ginger

salt and ground black pepper

3 Preheat the oven to 200°C/400°F/ Gas 6. Arrange the chicken pieces in a single layer on a non-stick baking sheet, brushing them with any extra sauce.

Variation Instead of chutney, try using the same quantity of tomato ketchup or mushroom ketchup.

4 Put the chicken pieces into the hot oven and cook for about 35 minutes until crisp, deep golden brown and cooked through (test by inserting a small sharp knife or skewer – the juices should run clear). Turn them over once or twice during cooking to encourage even browning.

1 With a sharp knife, make several deep slashes in the chicken pieces, cutting down to the bone.

2 In a large bowl, mix the oil, chutney, Worcestershire sauce, mustard, cayenne, ginger and seasoning. Add the chicken pieces and toss them in the mixture, until well coated. Cover and leave to stand for 1 hour.

Energy 299kcal/1254kJ; Protein 47.4g; Carbohydrate 0.3g, of which sugars 0.3g; Fat 12g, of which saturates 2.6g; Cholesterol 236mg; Calcium 41mg; Fibre 0.6g; Sodium 207mg

Roast goose with apples

The goose goes far back into the culinary history of England. Today it is a seasonal and costly treat that is popular at Christmas and New Year, but it was traditionally served on Michaelmas Day (29 September), having been fattened on barley stubble after the harvest, and it was said to bring financial luck to those who ate it then. Apples are in season at the same time and their fresh sharp flavour offsets the richness of the goose beautifully.

Serves 8

1 oven-ready goose weighing about 5.5kg/12lb, with giblets

1 small onion, sliced

2 small carrots, sliced

2 celery sticks, sliced

small bunch of parsley and thyme

450/1lb black pudding (blood sausage), crumbled or chopped

1 large garlic clove, crushed

2 large cooking apples, peeled, cored and finely chopped

250ml/8fl oz/1 cup dry (hard) cider

about 15ml/1 tbsp flour

salt and ground black pepper

roast potatoes and freshly cooked seasonal vegetables, to serve

1 Remove the goose liver from the giblets and put the the rest of the giblets into a pan with the onion, carrots, celery and herbs. Cover with cold water, season and simmer for 30–45 minutes to make a stock for the gravy, top up with water if necessary. Preheat the oven to 200°C/400°F/Gas 6.

Cook's tips When buying a goose, allow about 675g/1½lb per person.
• Save the copious fat that you drain from the goose during cooking and store in the refrigerator. It keeps for several weeks, and you can use it to roast the crispest, most delicious potatoes and parsnips for future meals.

2 Meanwhile, chop the liver finely and mix it with the black pudding, garlic and apples. Add salt and black pepper to the stuffing, then sprinkle in 75ml/2½fl oz/⅓ cup cider to bind it.

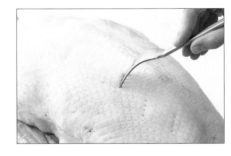

3 Wipe out the goose and stuff it with this mixture. Prick the skin all over with a fork, sprinkle generously with salt and pepper and rub in well.

4 Weigh the stuffed goose and calculate the correct cooking time at 15 minutes per 450g/1lb and 15 minutes over. Put the goose on a rack in a large roasting pan, cover with foil and put it into the preheated oven.

5 After 1 hour, remove the goose from the oven and carefully pour off the hot fat that has accumulated. Pour the remaining dry cider over the goose, replace the foil, and return to the oven.

6 Half an hour before the end of the estimated cooking time, remove the foil and baste the goose with the juices. Return to the oven, uncovered, and allow the skin to brown and crisp.

7 The goose is cooked if the juices run clear when the thickest part of the thigh is pierced with a skewer. Transfer the goose to a warmed serving plate, and rest in a warm place for at least 20 minutes before carving.

8 While the goose is resting, make the gravy. Pour off any excess fat from the roasting pan, leaving 30ml/2 tbsp, then sprinkle in enough flour to absorb it.

9 Cook over a medium heat for 1 minute, scraping the pan to loosen the sediment. Strain the giblet stock and stir in enough to make the gravy.

10 Bring the gravy to the boil and simmer for a few minutes, stirring constantly. Add any juices that have accumulated under the cooked goose, season to taste and pour the gravy into a heated sauceboat.

11 Carve the goose into slices at the table and serve with the gravy, roast potatoes and some seasonal vegetables.

Energy 822kcal/3437kJ; Protein 54.8g; Carbohydrate 44.1g, of which sugars 21.8g; Fat 48.7g, of which saturates 0.9g; Cholesterol 0mg; Calcium 87mg; Fibre 3.1g; Sodium 486mg

Duck with plum sauce

This is an updated version of an old English dish that was traditionally served in the late summer and early autumn, when Victoria plums are ripe and abundant. The sharp, fruity flavour of the plums balances the richness of the duck.

Serves 4

4 duck quarters

1 large red onion, finely chopped

500g/1¼lb ripe plums, quartered and stoned (pitted)

30ml/2 tbsp redcurrant jelly

salt and ground black pepper

1 Prick the duck skin all over with a fork to release the fat during cooking and help give a crisp result, then place the portions in a heavy frying pan, skin side down.

Cook's tip Make sure the plums are very ripe, otherwise the mixture may be too dry and the sauce extremely tart.

2 Cook the duck pieces for 10 minutes on each side, or until golden brown and cooked right through. Remove the duck from the frying pan, using tongs or a draining spoon, and keep warm.

Variations The red onion can be replaced with a white or a brown one.
• Fine cut orange marmalade makes a tangy alternative to the redcurrant jelly.

3 Pour away all but 30ml/2 tbsp of the duck fat, then stir-fry the onion for 5 minutes, or until golden. Add the plums and cook for a further 5 minutes, stirring. Add the redcurrant jelly.

4 Replace the duck portions and cook for a further 5 minutes or until thoroughly reheated. Season with salt and pepper to taste before serving.

Energy 608kcal/2515kJ; Protein 15.1g; Carbohydrate 17.4g, of which sugars 17g; Fat 53.5g, of which saturates 14.5g; Cholesterol 0mg; Calcium 35mg; Fibre 2.2g; Sodium 102mg

Pheasant with mushrooms, chestnuts and bacon

Braising is a slow, gentle cooking method, ideal for pheasants available at the end of the season, when they are no longer tender enough to roast but are full of flavour. Here they are cooked with mushrooms and chestnuts, which are in season at the same time.

Serves 4

2 mature pheasants

50g/2oz/4 tbsp butter

75ml/5 tbsp brandy

12 baby (pearl) onions, peeled

1 celery stick, chopped

50g/2oz unsmoked rindless bacon

45ml/3 tbsp plain (all-purpose) flour

550ml/18fl oz/2½ cups chicken stock

175g/6oz peeled, cooked chestnuts

350g/12oz/4 cups mixed wild mushrooms, trimmed and sliced

15ml/1 tbsp lemon juice

salt and ground black pepper

1 Preheat the oven to 160°C/325°F/Gas 3. Season the pheasants with salt and pepper. Melt half the butter in a large flameproof casserole and brown on all sides over a medium heat. Transfer them to a shallow roasting dish.

2 Pour off the excess fat from the casserole and return it to the heat. Add the brandy, stir to loosen the sediment, then pour over the pheasants.

3 Wipe out the casserole and melt the remaining butter. Cut the bacon into strips and brown in the butter with the onions and celery for 5 minutes. Sprinkle the flour into the casserole and cook, stirring, for 1 minute.

4 Gradually add the chicken stock, stirring until smooth. Add the chestnuts, mushrooms, the pheasants and their juices and bring back to a gentle simmer. Cover the dish, put into the hot oven and cook for 1½ hours or until the pheasants are tender.

5 Bring the sauce back to the boil, add the lemon juice and season to taste. Transfer the cooked pheasants and vegetables to a warmed serving plate. Pour over some of the sauce and serve the rest on the side.

Energy 883kcal/3699kJ; Protein 86.8g; Carbohydrate 32.3g, of which sugars 6.9g; Fat 41.6g, of which saturates 15.8g; Cholesterol 35mg; Calcium 205mg; Fibre 2.9g; Sodium 920mg

Roast pheasant with game chips

The game season begins on 1 October, when hen pheasants are in their prime. The addition of bacon, covering the breast, helps to keep the moisture in the roasted meat. Crisp-fried game chips are the traditional, and perfect, accompaniment.

Serves 2

1 hen pheasant

25g/1oz/2 tbsp butter

115g/4oz rindless streaky (fatty) bacon rashers (strips)

2 medium potatoes

oil, for deep-frying

salt and ground black pepper

For the stuffing

25g/1oz/2 tbsp butter

1 leek, chopped

115g/4oz peeled, cooked chestnuts, coarsely chopped (see Cook's tip)

30ml/2 tbsp chopped fresh flat-leaf parsley

For the gravy

15ml/1 tbsp cornflour (cornstarch)

300ml/½ pint/1¼ cups well-flavoured chicken stock

50ml/2fl oz/¼ cup port

1 Preheat the oven to 190°C/375°F/ Gas 5. Pick any stray quills or stubs of feathers from the pheasant and season the bird inside and out with salt and black pepper.

Cook's tip For convenience, use vacuum-packed or frozen chestnuts rather than fresh, which are fiddly to peel and cook. Simply rinse the chestnuts thoroughly with boiling water and drain before using. Whole, unsweetened canned chestnuts could be used, but they tend to be fairly dense and can be soft.

2 Carefully loosen and lift the skin covering the breast and rub the butter between the skin and flesh.

3 To make the stuffing, melt the butter in a pan and cook the leek for about 5 minutes until softened but not coloured. Remove from the heat and mix in the chopped chestnuts, parsley and seasoning to taste.

4 Spoon the stuffing into the cavity of the pheasant and secure the opening with skewers. Arrange the bacon over the breast and place in a roasting pan.

5 Put into the hot oven and cook for 1–1½ hours, or until the juices run clear when the bird is pierced with a skewer in the thickest part of the leg.

6 Lift out and cover closely with foil, then leave to stand in a warm place for 15 minutes before carving.

7 On the stove, heat the juices in the roasting pan and stir in the cornflour. Gradually stir in the stock and port. Bring to the boil, then reduce the heat and simmer for about 5 minutes, until the sauce is slightly thickened and glossy. Strain the sauce and keep warm.

8 Peel the potatoes and cut into matchsticks. Heat the oil in a deep-fat fryer or large pan to 190°C/375°F and fry the chips until crisp, golden and cooked through. Drain on kitchen paper.

9 Serve the pheasant with the gravy and game chips.

Energy 897kcal/3742kJ; Protein 70.6g; Carbohydrate 34.3g, of which sugars 9.1g; Fat 50.8g, of which saturates 20g; Cholesterol 524mg; Calcium 127mg; Fibre 4.5g; Sodium 946mg

Vegetable Dishes and Salads

Home-grown vegetables, from beneath the soil and above, are enjoyed in a myriad of dishes. England is home to the kitchen garden of the great country estates, with its neatly laid-out beds interspersed with herbs and flowers; the back garden with wigwams of runner beans and rows of potatoes; and city allotments filled with everything from artichokes to pumpkins.

Pease pudding

"Pease pudding hot, pease pudding cold, pease pudding in the pot, nine days old ..." goes the old rhyme. This dish probably dates back to the 17th century, when puddings were boiled, wrapped in a cloth, in a pot alongside meat (usually bacon). Once a nationwide staple, it is still popular in the north-east. Needless to say, it is good with pork or bacon.

Serves 6

450g/1lb dried split yellow peas

40g/1½ oz/3 tbsp butter, cut into pieces

1 egg, lightly beaten

salt and ground black pepper

1 Cover the split peas with cold water and leave to soak for several hours or overnight.

2 Drain the peas and put them into a pan. Cover with fresh cold water, bring to the boil and simmer gently for about 45 minutes or until very soft.

3 Preheat the oven to 180°C/350°F/ Gas 4. Drain and purée the peas in a food processor or blender. Add the butter, egg and seasoning, mix, and spoon into a buttered ovenproof dish.

4 Put the dish into the hot oven and cook for about 30 minutes until the pudding is set.

Cook's tips Pease pudding can be steamed in a pudding bowl, securely covered with baking parchment and foil, for about 45 minutes.
• A small handful of chopped fresh mint or a pinch of dried mint can be added to the purée in step 3.

Mushy peas

Dried marrowfat peas, cooked and served in their own juice, are believed to have originated in the north of England. Today, they are popular all over the country, especially with fish and chips. In the West Riding of Yorkshire mushy peas are served with pork pie.

Serves 4–6

250g/9oz dried peas

1 small onion

1 small carrot

2.5ml/½ tsp sugar

25g/1oz/2 tbsp butter

salt and ground black pepper

1 Put the peas in a bowl and pour over boiling water to cover them well. Soak for about 12 hours or overnight.

2 Drain and rinse the peas and put into a pan. Add the onion, carrot, sugar and 600ml/1pint/2½ cups cold water. Bring to the boil and simmer gently for about 20 minutes or until the peas are soft and the water absorbed.

3 Remove the onion and carrot from the pan. Mash the peas, seasoning to taste with salt and black pepper, and stir in the butter.

Cook's tip Cooking the peas in a muslin (cheesecloth) bag in step 2 stops them disintegrating.

Energy 300kcal/1270kJ; Protein 18.9g; Carbohydrate 42.3g, of which sugars 1.8g; Fat 7.4g, of which saturates 3.9g; Cholesterol 46mg; Calcium 44mg; Fibre 3.7g; Sodium 79mg
Energy 68kcal/288kJ; Protein 4.8g; Carbohydrate 11.5g, of which sugars 1.4g; Fat 0.6g, of which saturates 0.1g; Cholesterol 0mg; Calcium 12mg; Fibre 1.5g; Sodium 283mg

Broad beans with bacon and mint

In early summer, tender young broad beans are a treat, and fresh mint and a smattering of crisply cooked bacon are their perfect partners. At other times of year, this recipe works well with frozen broad beans. Serve warm or at room temperature as a salad with crusty bread, or hot as an accompaniment to roast duck or chicken.

Serves 4–6

30ml/2 tbsp olive oil

175g/6oz streaky (fatty) bacon, cut into narrow strips

1 medium onion, thinly sliced

2.5ml/½ tsp sugar

450g/1lb shelled broad (fava) beans

15ml/1 tbsp cider vinegar

small handful of fresh mint, finely chopped

salt and ground black pepper

3 Meanwhile, bring a pan of water to the boil and add the beans. Cook for 5–8 minutes until tender. Drain well.

4 Add the cooked beans and bacon to the onions. Stir in the remaining oil, vinegar, seasonings and mint and serve.

1 Heat half the oil in a large pan and cook the bacon until crisp. Lift out with a slotted spoon and set aside.

2 Add the onion to the hot pan with the sugar and cook over a medium heat until soft and golden brown.

Energy 162kcal/674kJ; Protein 7.9g; Carbohydrate 9.6g, of which sugars 1.8g; Fat 10.5g, of which saturates 2.2g; Cholesterol 9mg; Calcium 45mg; Fibre 4.5g; Sodium 190mg

Braised red cabbage

In the English culinary tradition red cabbage has usually been pickled. However, it is a robust winter vegetable that takes on a beautiful colour and texture when cooked slowly and gently. This spiced version goes particularly well with pork, duck or game.

Serves 4–6

1kg/2¼lb red cabbage

2 onions, chopped

2 cooking apples, peeled, cored and coarsely grated

5ml/1 tsp freshly grated nutmeg

1.5ml/¼ tsp ground cloves

1.5ml/¼ tsp ground cinnamon

15ml/1 tbsp dark brown sugar

45ml/3 tbsp cider vinegar

25g/1oz/2 tbsp butter, cut into small pieces

salt and ground black pepper

1 Preheat the oven to 160°C/325°F/ Gas 3. Remove the large white ribs from the outer cabbage leaves, then shred the cabbage finely.

Cook's tip The braised cabbage can be cooked in advance and reheated in the oven for 30 minutes when needed. Leftovers can also be frozen.

2 Layer the shredded cabbage in a large ovenproof dish with the onions, apples, spices, sugar and seasoning. Pour the vinegar over and dot with the butter.

3 Cover, put into the hot oven and cook for about 1½ hours, stirring a couple of times, until the cabbage is very tender. Serve hot.

Energy 74kcal/309kJ; Protein 2.1g; Carbohydrate 10.1g, of which sugars 9.5g; Fat 3g, of which saturates 0.4g; Cholesterol 0mg; Calcium 53mg; Fibre 3.1g; Sodium 38mg

Roast beetroot with horseradish cream

Beetroot was very popular in Elizabethan days, when its vibrant colour was added to elaborate salads. In this recipe, its sweet flavour is enhanced first by roasting and then by the horseradish and vinegar in the cream. Serve it with roast beef or venison.

Serves 4–6

10–12 small whole beetroot

30ml/2 tbsp oil

45ml/3 tbsp grated fresh horseradish

15ml/1 tbsp white wine vinegar

10ml/2 tsp caster (superfine) sugar

150ml/¼ pint/⅔ cup double (heavy) cream

salt

Cook's tips If you are unable to find any fresh horseradish root use preserved grated horseradish instead.
• For a lighter sauce, replace half the cream with thick plain yogurt.

1 Preheat the oven to 180°C/350°F/ Gas 4. Wash the beetroot without breaking their skins. Trim the stalks very short but do not remove them completely. Toss the beetroot in the oil and sprinkle with salt. Spread them in a roasting pan and cover with foil. Put into the hot oven and cook for about 1½ hours or until soft throughout. Leave to cool, covered, for 10 minutes.

2 Meanwhile, make the horseradish sauce. Put the horseradish, vinegar and sugar into a bowl and mix well. Whip the cream until thickened and fold in the horseradish mixture. Cover and chill until required.

3 When the beetroot are cool enough to handle, slip off the skins and serve with the sauce.

Energy 254kcal/1052kJ; Protein 2.1g; Carbohydrate 10g, of which sugars 9.1g; Fat 22.2g, of which saturates 3.2g; Cholesterol 1mg; Calcium 26mg; Fibre 2.3g; Sodium 143mg

Roast parsnips with honey and nutmeg

The Romans considered parsnips to be a luxury, at which time they were credited with a variety of medicinal and aphrodisiac qualities. Today, they are especially enjoyed when roasted around a joint of beef. Their sweetness mingles well with spices and honey.

Serves 4–6

4 medium parsnips

30ml/2 tbsp plain (all-purpose) flour seasoned with salt and pepper

60ml/4 tbsp oil

15–30ml/1–2 tbsp clear honey

freshly grated nutmeg

1 Preheat the oven to 200°C/400°F/ Gas 6. Peel the parsnips and cut each one lengthways into quarters, removing any woody cores. Drop into a pan of boiling water and cook for 5 minutes until slightly softened.

2 Drain the parsnips thoroughly, then toss in the seasoned flour, shaking off any excess.

3 Pour the oil into a roasting pan and put into the oven until hot. Add the parsnips, tossing them in the oil and arranging them in a single layer.

4 Return the pan to the oven and cook the parsnips for about 30 minutes, turning occasionally, until crisp, golden brown and cooked through.

5 Drizzle with the honey and sprinkle a little grated nutmeg. Return the parsnips to the oven for 5 minutes before serving.

Parsnip chips

Before sugar was available, parsnips were used to sweeten cakes and jams. By the 20th century they had become an everyday item and were even dried to make "coffee" during World War II. These chips are particularly good served with grilled chicken or sausages.

Serves 4

oil, for deep frying

2 large parsnips

30ml/2 tbsp plain (all-purpose) flour

salt

good pinch of curry powder (optional)

Variation For thicker chips, cut the parsnips lengthwise into wedges, removing any woody core, and boil until almost tender, then flour them and deep-fry.

1 Heat the oil to about 180°C/350°F. Season the flour with salt and curry powder, if using.

2 Peel the parsnips and, using a potato peeler, cut lengthways into thin strips. Put them into a pan, cover with water and bring just to the boil. Drain and dry thoroughly, then toss the strips in the seasoned flour.

3 Fry the strips, in batches, in the hot oil until crisp and golden brown outside and soft inside. Lift out and drain on kitchen paper. Sprinkle with a little salt and curry powder (if using) to serve.

Energy 144kcal/600kJ; Protein 2g; Carbohydrate 16.2g, of which sugars 6.7g; Fat 8.3g, of which saturates 1g; Cholesterol 0mg; Calcium 41mg; Fibre 4g; Sodium 9mg

Energy 230kcal/956kJ; Protein 2.3g; Carbohydrate 16.8g, of which sugars 5.1g; Fat 17.6g, of which saturates 2.1g; Cholesterol 0mg; Calcium 47mg; Fibre 4.3g; Sodium 9mg

Potatoes and parsnips with garlic and cream

For the best results, cut the potatoes and parsnips very thinly – use a mandolin if you have one. This method is also ideal for cooking sweet potatoes, which Tudor cooks would have been more likely to slice and crystallize, to serve as a sweetmeat.

Serves 4–6

3 large potatoes, total weight about 675g/1½lb

350g/12oz small to medium-sized parsnips

200ml/7fl oz/scant 1 cup single (light) cream

100ml/3½fl oz/scant ½ cup milk

2 garlic cloves, crushed

butter, for greasing

about 5ml/1 tsp freshly grated nutmeg

75g/3oz/¾ cup coarsely grated Cheddar or Red Leicester cheese

salt and ground black pepper

4 Arrange the potatoes and parsnips in the dish, sprinkling each layer with a little freshly grated nutmeg, salt and ground black pepper

5 Pour the liquid into the dish and press the potatoes and parsnips down into it. Cover with lightly buttered foil and cook in the hot oven for 45 minutes.

6 Remove the foil and sprinkle the grated cheese over the vegetables in an even layer.

7 Return the dish to the oven and continue cooking, uncovered, for a further 20–30 minutes, or until the potatoes and parsnips are tender and the top is golden brown.

1 Peel the potatoes and parsnips and cut them into thin slices. Cook in a large pan of salted boiling water for 5 minutes. Drain and cool slightly.

2 Meanwhile, pour the cream and milk into a heavy pan and add the crushed garlic. Bring to the boil over a medium heat, then remove from the heat and leave to stand for about 10 minutes.

3 Preheat the oven to 180°C/350°F/ Gas 4 and lightly butter the bottom and sides of a shallow ovenproof dish.

Energy 241kcal/1012kJ; Protein 7.8g; Carbohydrate 27.2g, of which sugars 6.4g; Fat 11.7g, of which saturates 7.2g; Cholesterol 31mg; Calcium 173mg; Fibre 3.9g; Sodium 126mg

Warm potato salad with bacon dressing

This tasty summer salad becomes a favourite with all who try it. Choose dry-cured bacon and real new-season potatoes rather than all-year "baby" potatoes, if possible. Using superior ingredients makes this a special dish, and it's ideal for a barbecue or party.

Serves 4–6

900g/2lb small new potatoes

sprig of mint

15–30ml/1–2 tbsp olive oil

1 onion, thinly sliced

175g/6oz smoked bacon, cut into small strips

2 garlic cloves, crushed

30ml/2 tbsp chopped fresh parsley

1 small bunch of chives, chopped

15ml/1 tbsp wine vinegar or cider vinegar

15ml/1 tbsp wholegrain mustard

salt and ground black pepper

1 Scrape the new potatoes and cook in salted water with the mint for about 10 minutes, until just tender. Drain and cool a little, then tip into a salad bowl.

2 Heat the oil in a frying pan, add the onion and cook gently until just softening, stirring occasionally. Add the bacon to the pan and cook for 3–5 minutes, until it begins to crisp.

3 Add the garlic and cook for another minute or so, then remove from the heat and add the chopped herbs, vinegar, mustard and seasoning to taste, remembering that the bacon may be salty.

4 Pour the dressing over the potatoes. Toss gently to mix, and serve the salad while still warm.

Energy 318kcal/1319kJ; Protein 12.4g; Carbohydrate 10.9g, of which sugars 2.2g; Fat 25.4g, of which saturates 4g; Cholesterol 198mg; Calcium 106mg; Fibre 2.3g; Sodium 268mg

Savoury potato cakes

Make these crisp cakes of grated potato as small or as large as you like. The addition of a little bacon makes them extra appetizing. Serve them just as they are, with a mixed salad and a spoonful of thick yogurt, or as an accompaniment to fish.

Serves 4

450g/1lb potatoes, grated, rinsed, drained and dried

1 small onion, grated

3 rashers (slices) streaky (fatty) bacon, finely chopped

30ml/2 tbsp self-raising (self-rising) flour

2 eggs, beaten

oil, for frying

salt and ground black pepper

1 Mix the potatoes with the onion, bacon, flour, eggs and seasoning.

2 Heat 1cm/½in oil in a frying pan, then add about 15ml/1 tbsp of the potato mixture and spread it slightly with the back of the spoon.

3 Add a few more spoonfuls, leaving space between them, and cook for 4–5 minutes, until golden underneath.

4 Turn the cakes over and cook for 3–4 minutes until golden brown and cooked through. Keep warm while you cook the remaining potato mixture.

Pan haggerty

This traditional Northumberland dish works best with firm-fleshed potatoes such as Cara, Desirée or Maris Piper. Serve it cut into wedges or spoon it straight out of the pan.

Serves 4

60ml/4 tbsp oil

450g/1lb firm potatoes, thinly sliced

1 large onion, thinly sliced

115g/4oz/1 cup grated mature Cheddar cheese

salt and ground black pepper

1 Heat the oil in a large, heavy frying pan. Remove the pan from the heat and add alternate layers of potato, onion slices and cheese, starting and ending with potatoes, and seasoning each layer as you go. Replace the pan over a low heat.

2 Cook for 30 minutes, until the potatoes are soft and the underside has browned. Meanwhile, preheat the grill (broiler).

3 Place the pan under the grill for 5–10 minutes to brown the top. Slide the potatoes onto a warmed plate to serve.

Energy 186kcal/776kJ; Protein 6g; Carbohydrate 12.3g, of which sugars 1.2g; Fat 12.6g, of which saturates 4.2g; Cholesterol 38mg; Calcium 126mg; Fibre 1g; Sodium 246mg

Energy 271kcal/1128kJ; Protein 9.8g; Carbohydrate 21.1g, of which sugars 3.6g; Fat 16.9g, of which saturates 7.5g; Cholesterol 30mg; Calcium 215mg; Fibre 1.7g; Sodium 206mg

Savoury Pastry

Pastry is a passion with the English, whether it's a portable feast in the shape of an individual Cornish pasty; a traditional chicken pie that feeds and cheers the family; or an elegant dish, such as asparagus flan or raised game pie for a sophisticated dinner. Each region and period in history has its own variation and favourite.

Steak and oyster pie

In the 17th century, oysters were so plentiful and cheap that not only could the poor afford to eat them, they were even used to feed animals. When enormous beef pies were prepared for large gatherings, oysters were added to make the beef go further. Though oysters are a luxury today, they add a wonderful flavour to the filling in this pie.

Serves 6

30ml/2 tbsp plain (all-purpose) flour

1kg/2¼lb rump (round) steak, cut into 5cm/2in pieces

45ml/3 tbsp oil

25g/1oz/2 tbsp butter

1 large onion, chopped

300ml/½ pint/1¼ cups beef stock

300ml/½ pint/1¼ cups brown ale or red wine

30ml/2 tbsp fresh thyme leaves

225g/8oz chestnut mushrooms, halved if large

12 shelled oysters

375g/13oz puff pastry, thawed if frozen

beaten egg, to glaze

salt and ground black pepper

1 Preheat the oven if using (see step 3) to 150°C/300°F/Gas 2. Season the flour with salt and pepper and toss the pieces of steak in it until well coated. Heat half the oil with half the butter in a large pan or flameproof casserole and quickly brown the meat in batches. Set it to one side.

2 Add the remaining oil and butter to the hot pan, stir in the chopped onion and cook over a medium heat, stirring occasionally, until golden brown and beginning to soften.

3 Return the meat and any juices to the pan and stir in the stock, ale or wine and thyme. Bring just to the boil then cover the pan and either simmer very gently on the stove or cook in the preheated oven for about 1½ hours, or until the beef is tender.

4 Using a slotted spoon, lift the meat and onion out of the liquid and put it into a 1.75 litre/3 pint/7½ cup pie dish. Bring the liquid to the boil and reduce to about 600ml/1 pint/2½ cups.

Cook's tip Though using rump steak for the pie is traditional, replacing it with the same amount of braising steak is acceptable.

5 Season to taste and stir in the mushrooms, then pour the mixture over the meat in the dish. Leave to cool. Preheat the oven to 200°C/400°F/Gas 6, if not already using.

6 Add the oysters to the cooled meat, pushing them down into the mixture.

7 Roll out the pastry on a lightly floured surface to a shape 2.5cm/1in larger than the dish. Trim off a 1cm/½in strip all around the edge. Brush the rim of the dish with a little beaten egg and lay the strip on it. Brush the strip with egg, lay the pastry sheet over the top, trim to fit and press the edges together well to seal them. Brush the top of the pie with beaten egg.

8 Put the pie into the hot oven and cook for about 40 minutes, until the pastry is crisp and golden brown and the filling is piping hot.

Energy 689kcal/2874kJ; Protein 49.4g; Carbohydrate 29.8g, of which sugars 1g; Fat 39g, of which saturates 9.1g; Cholesterol 144mg; Calcium 145mg; Fibre 0.4g; Sodium 674mg

Veal and ham pie

In the cold version of veal and ham pie, the filling is completely enclosed in hot water crust pastry. In this hot version, the pastry sits on top of the classic combination of meat and eggs, keeping the contents moist and the aromas sealed in until the pie is cut open.

Serves 4

450g/1lb boneless shoulder of veal, cut into cubes

225g/8oz lean gammon, cut into cubes

15ml/1 tbsp plain (all-purpose) flour

large pinch each of dry mustard and ground black pepper

25g/1oz/2 tbsp butter

15ml/1 tbsp oil

1 onion, chopped

600ml/1 pint/2½ cups chicken or veal stock

2 eggs, hard-boiled and sliced

30ml/2 tbsp chopped fresh parsley

For the pastry

175g/6oz/1½ cups plain (all-purpose) flour

pinch of salt

85g/3oz/6 tbsp butter, diced

beaten egg, to glaze

1 Preheat the oven to 180°C/350°F/ Gas 4. Mix the veal and gammon in a bowl. Season the flour with the mustard and black pepper, then add it to the meat and toss well.

2 Heat the butter and oil in a large, flameproof casserole until sizzling, then cook the meat mixture in batches until golden on all sides. Use a slotted spoon to remove the meat and set aside.

3 Cook the onion in the fat remaining in the casserole until softened but not coloured. Stir in the stock and the meat. Cover and cook in the hot oven for 1½ hours or until the veal is tender. Adjust the seasoning and leave to cool.

4 To make the pastry, sift the flour into a bowl with the salt and rub in the butter until the mixture resembles fine crumbs. Mix in just enough cold water to bind the mixture, gathering it together with your fingertips. Wrap the pastry in clear film (plastic wrap), and chill for at least 30 minutes.

Variation Use ready-made fresh or frozen puff pastry to cover the pie.

5 Spoon the veal mixture into a 1.5 litre/2½ pint/6¼ cup pie dish. Arrange the slices of hard-boiled egg on top and sprinkle with the parsley.

6 On a lightly floured surface, roll out the pastry to about 4cm/1½in larger than the top of the pie dish. Cut a strip from around the edge, dampen the rim of the dish and press the pastry strip on to it. Brush the pastry rim with beaten egg and top with the lid.

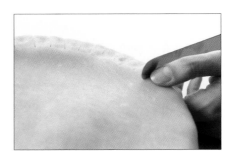

7 Trim off any excess pastry. Use the blunt edge of a knife to tap the outside edge, pressing the pastry down with your finger to seal in the filling. Pinch the pastry between your fingers to flute the edge. Roll out any trimmings and cut out shapes to decorate the pie.

8 Brush the top of the pie with beaten egg, put into the hot oven and cook for 30–40 minutes or until the pastry is well risen and golden brown. Serve hot.

Energy 621kcal/2595kJ; Protein 42.4g; Carbohydrate 39.2g, of which sugars 2.6g; Fat 33.8g, of which saturates 17.2g; Cholesterol 281mg; Calcium 128mg; Fibre 2.3g; Sodium 1007mg

Chicken and ham pie

This pie has pastry top and bottom. Though it can be served warm, it is even more delicious cold. Serve it with salad for a summer lunch or take it on a picnic.

Serves 6

For the pastry

275g/10oz/2½ cups plain (all-purpose) flour

pinch of salt

150g/5oz/⅔ cup butter, diced

For the filling

800g/1¾lb chicken breast

350g/12oz smoked or cured ham

6 spring onions (scallions), chopped

15ml/1 tbsp chopped fresh tarragon

10ml/2 tsp chopped fresh thyme

grated rind and juice of ½ lemon

60ml/4 tbsp double (heavy) cream

5ml/1 tsp ground mace or nutmeg

beaten egg, to glaze

salt and ground black pepper

1 Sift the flour into a bowl with the salt and rub in the butter until the mixture resembles fine crumbs. Mix in just enough cold water to bind the mixture, gathering it together with your fingertips. Chill for 30 minutes.

2 Preheat the oven to 190°C/375°F/ Gas 5. Roll out one-third of the pastry.

3 Line a 20cm/8in pie dish 5cm/2in deep with the pastry and place on a baking (cookie) sheet.

4 Mince (grind) or process 115g/4oz of the chicken with the gammon. Place the meat in a bowl and add the spring onions, tarragon and thyme, lemon rind, 15ml/1 tbsp lemon juice and seasoning. Stir well, adding enough cream to make a soft mixture.

5 Cut the remaining chicken into 1cm/½in pieces and mix with the remaining lemon juice, the mace or nutmeg and seasoning.

6 Put one-third of the gammon mixture in the pastry base and cover with half the chopped chicken. Repeat the layers, then top with the remaining gammon.

7 Dampen the edges of the pastry base. Roll out the remaining pastry and cover the pie, sealing the edges firmly.

8 Use the trimmings to decorate the top. Make a small hole in the centre and brush with beaten egg. Cook for 20 minutes then turn the oven down to 160°C/325°F/Gas 3 and cook for a further 1–1¼ hours. Cover with foil if the pastry becomes too brown.

Energy 431kcal/1804kJ; Protein 34.8g; Carbohydrate 23.8g, of which sugars 0.8g; Fat 22.5g, of which saturates 8.3g; Cholesterol 98mg; Calcium 57mg; Fibre 1.1g; Sodium 648mg

Game pie

Raised game pie makes an impressive centrepiece, especially if made in a fluted raised pie mould. Not only does it look magnificent, it tastes wonderful. These pies used to be made in the country and sent to London for Christmas, so the crust had to be stoutly built.

Serves 10

25g/1oz/2 tbsp butter

1 onion, finely chopped

2 garlic cloves, finely chopped

900g/2lb mixed boneless game, such as pheasant and/or pigeon breast, venison and rabbit, diced

30ml/2 tbsp chopped fresh herbs such as parsley, thyme and marjoram

salt and ground black pepper

For the pâté

50g/2oz/¼ cup butter

2 garlic cloves, finely chopped

450g/1lb chicken livers, rinsed, trimmed and chopped

60ml/4 tbsp brandy

5ml/1 tsp ground mace

For the hot water crust pastry

675g/1½lb/6 cups strong plain (all-purpose) flour

5ml/1 tsp salt

115ml/3½fl oz/scant ½ cup milk

115ml/3½fl oz/scant ½ cup water

115g/4oz/½ cup lard, diced

115g/4oz/½ cup butter, diced

beaten egg, to glaze

For the jelly

300ml/½ pint/1¼ cups game or beef consommé

2.5ml/½ tsp powdered gelatine

1 Melt the butter until foaming and cook the onion and garlic until softened but not coloured. Remove from the heat and mix with the meat and herbs. Season well, cover and chill.

2 To make the pâté, melt the butter in a pan until foaming, add the garlic and chicken livers and cook until just browned. Remove from the heat and stir in the brandy and mace. Purée the mixture in a blender or food processor until smooth, then leave to cool.

3 To make the pastry, sift the flour and salt into a bowl and make a well in the centre. Gently heat the milk, water, lard and butter together until melted. Bring to the boil, removing from the heat as soon as the mixture begins to bubble. Pour the hot liquid into the well in the flour and beat until smooth. Cover and leave until cool enough to handle.

4 Preheat the oven to 200°C/400°F/Gas 6. Roll out two-thirds of the pastry and use to line a 23cm/9in raised pie mould, pressing it in with your fingers. Spoon in half the game mixture and press it down evenly. Add the pâté, then top with the remaining game.

Cook's tip If you don't have a raised pie mould, use a 20cm/8in springform cake tin (pan).

5 Roll out the remaining pastry to form a lid. Brush the edge of the pastry lining the tin with a little water and cover the pie with the lid. Trim off excess pastry and pinch the edges together to seal. Make two holes in the centre of the lid and brush the top with egg. Use the trimmings to roll out leaves to garnish the pie and brush them with egg.

6 Put into the hot oven and cook for 20 minutes, then cover with foil and cook for 10 minutes. Reduce the oven temperature to 150°C/300°F/Gas 2. Brush the pie again with egg and cook for a further 1½ hours, keeping the top covered loosely with foil.

7 Remove from the oven and leave to stand for 15 minutes. Increase the oven temperature to 200°C/400°F/Gas 6. Stand the tin on a baking sheet and remove its sides. Quickly brush the sides of the pie with beaten egg, cover the top with foil, then cook for another 15 minutes to brown the sides. Leave to cool completely, then chill overnight.

8 To make the jelly, heat the consommé in a small pan until hot but not boiling, whisk in the gelatine until dissolved and leave to cool until just setting. Using a small funnel, carefully pour the jellied consommé into the holes in the pie. Chill until set.

Energy 448kcal/1871kJ; Protein 28.3g; Carbohydrate 29.5g, of which sugars 5.3g; Fat 24.9g, of which saturates 9.5g; Cholesterol 55mg; Calcium 67mg; Fibre 1.5g; Sodium 393mg

Cheese and asparagus flan

The English asparagus season is short, so you need to make the most of it. The distinctive taste of fresh asparagus comes through in this flan and makes a small amount go further. It has an affinity with cheese, with each ingredient enhancing the flavour of the other.

Serves 5–6

175g/6oz/1½ cups plain (all-purpose) flour

pinch of salt

40g/1½oz/3 tbsp lard, diced

40g/1½oz/3 tbsp butter, diced

300g/11oz small asparagus spears weighed after trimming

75g/3oz mature Cheddar cheese, grated

3 spring onions (scallions), thinly sliced

2 eggs

300ml/½ pint/1¼ cups double (heavy) cream

freshly grated nutmeg

salt and ground black pepper

1 To make the pastry, sift the flour and salt into a bowl and add the lard and butter. With your fingertips, rub the fats into the flour until the mixture resembles fine breadcrumbs.

2 Stir in about 45ml/3 tbsp cold water until the mixture can be gathered together into a ball of dough. (Or use a food processor.) Wrap the pastry and chill for 30 minutes.

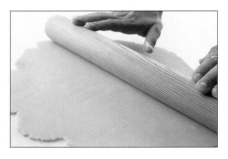

3 Put a flat baking sheet in the oven and preheat to 200°C/400°F/Gas 6. Roll out the pastry on a lightly floured work surface and use it to line a 20cm/8in flan tin (pan).

4 Line the pastry case (pie shell) with baking parchment or foil and add a layer of baking beans. Put the flan tin on to the heated baking sheet in the oven and cook for 10–15 minutes until set. Carefully remove the beans and parchment or foil, return the pastry to the oven and cook for a further 5 minutes, until light golden brown on the edges. Remove the flan and reduce the temperature to 180°C/350°F/Gas 4.

5 Meanwhile, cook the asparagus spears in lightly salted boiling water for 2–3 minutes or until only just tender. Drain, rinse under cold water and dry on kitchen paper. Cut the asparagus spears into 2.5cm/1in lengths, leaving the tips whole.

6 Scatter half the cheese in the base of the cooked pastry case and add the asparagus and the spring onions.

7 Beat the eggs with the cream and season with salt, pepper and nutmeg.

8 Pour over the asparagus and top with the remaining cheese.

9 Return the flan to the hot baking sheet in the oven and cook for about 30 minutes or until just set. Leave the flan to settle for 5 minutes before cutting and serving.

Energy 547kcal/2266kJ; Protein 10.4g; Carbohydrate 24.7g, of which sugars 2.4g; Fat 45.6g, of which saturates 26.2g; Cholesterol 165mg; Calcium 184mg; Fibre 1.8g; Sodium 167mg

Puddings and Desserts

Everyone loves a pudding, and the English have many variations to enjoy, even if it's only as an occasional treat. Orchard fruits are often a main ingredient – stewed or baked and made into tarts, crumbles and pies. There are also nursery-style puds made with sponge, suet pastry, bread, rice or batter, as well as rich, creamy concoctions made with products from the dairy.

Energy 700kcal/2919kJ; Protein 10.8g; Carbohydrate 57.1g, of which sugars 36.7g; Fat 49.9g, of which saturates 17.1g; Cholesterol 257mg; Calcium 110mg; Fibre 0.9g; Sodium 394mg

Lemon meringue pie

This popular dessert is a 20th-century development of older English cheesecakes – open tarts with a filling of curds. It was particularly relished in the 1950s after the years of wartime rationing, when sugar, lemons and eggs became plentiful once more. The pie is best served at room temperature, with or without cream.

Serves 6

For the pastry

115g/4oz/1 cup plain (all-purpose) flour

pinch of salt

25g/1oz/2 tbsp lard, diced

25g/1oz/2 tbsp butter, diced

For the filling

50g/2oz/¼ cup cornflour (cornstarch)

175g/6oz/¾ cup caster (superfine) sugar

finely grated rind and juice of 2 lemons

2 egg yolks

15g/½oz/1 tbsp butter, diced

For the meringue topping

2 egg whites

75g/3oz/½ cup caster (superfine) sugar

1 To make the pastry, sift the flour and salt into a bowl and add the lard and butter. With the fingertips, lightly rub the fats into the flour until the mixture resembles fine crumbs.

2 Stir in about 20ml/2 tbsp cold water until the mixture can be gathered together into a smooth ball of dough. (Alternatively make the pastry using a food processor.) Wrap the pastry and refrigerate for at least 30 minutes. Meanwhile, preheat the oven to 200°C/400°F/Gas 6.

3 Roll out the pastry on a lightly floured surface and use to line a 20cm/8in flan tin (pan). Prick the base with a fork, line with baking parchment or foil and add a layer of baking beans to prevent the pastry rising.

4 Put the pastry case (pie shell) into the hot oven and cook for 15 minutes. Remove the beans and parchment or foil, return the pastry to the oven and cook for a further 5 minutes until crisp and golden brown. Reduce the oven temperature to 150°C/300°F/Gas 2.

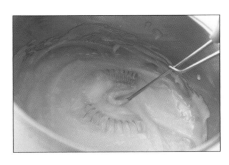

5 To make the lemon filling, put the cornflour into a pan and add the sugar, lemon rind and 300ml/½ pint/ 1¼ cups water. Heat the mixture, stirring continuously, until it comes to the boil and thickens. Reduce the heat and simmer very gently for 1 minute. Remove the pan from the heat and stir in the lemon juice.

6 Add the the egg yolks to the lemon mixture, one at a time and beating after each addition, and then stir in the butter. Tip the mixture into the baked pastry case and level the surface.

7 To make the meringue topping, whisk the egg whites until stiff peaks form then whisk in half the sugar. Fold in the rest of the sugar using a metal spoon.

8 Spread the meringue over the lemon filling, covering it completely. Cook for about 20 minutes until lightly browned.

Energy 357kcal/1497kJ; Protein 6.8g; Carbohydrate 42.8g, of which sugars 25.1g; Fat 18.9g, of which saturates 9g; Cholesterol 129mg; Calcium 108mg; Fibre 0.7g; Sodium 137mg

Treacle tart

The name of this tart is somewhat misleading, since golden syrup, not treacle or molasses, is used for the filling. Golden syrup became available only in the late 19th century, making this plate tart a relatively recent invention. Serve it warm or cold, with custard or cream.

3 Mix the breadcrumbs with the ginger, if using, and spread the mixture over the bottom of the pastry. Gently warm the syrup with the lemon rind and juice (on the stove or in the microwave) until quite runny and pour evenly over the breadcrumbs.

4 Gather the reserved pastry trimmings into a ball, roll out on a lightly floured surface and cut into long, narrow strips. Twist these into spirals and arrange them in a lattice pattern on top of the tart, pressing them on to the edge to secure. Trim the ends.

Serves 6

175g/6oz/1½ cups plain (all-purpose) flour

pinch of salt

40g/1½oz/3 tbsp lard

40g/1½oz/3 tbsp butter, diced

75g/3oz/1½ cups fresh breadcrumbs

2.5ml/½ tsp ground ginger (optional)

225g/8oz/1 cup golden (corn) syrup

grated rind and juice of 1 lemon

1 Sift the flour and salt into a bowl and add the lard and butter. With the fingertips, rub the fats into the flour until the mixture resembles fine breadcrumbs. Stir in about 45ml/3 tbsp cold water until the mixture can be gathered together into a smooth ball of dough. Wrap the pastry and refrigerate for 30 minutes. Meanwhile, preheat the oven to 190°C/375°F/Gas 5.

2 Roll out the pastry on a lightly floured surface and use to line a 20cm/8in flan tin (pan) or pie plate, reserving the trimmings.

5 Put into the hot oven and cook for about 25 minutes until the pastry is golden brown and cooked through and the filling has set.

Variation Omit the lemon rind and juice if you prefer. Sometimes finely crushed cornflakes are used in place of the breadcrumbs.

Energy 420kcal/1764kJ; Protein 4.1g; Carbohydrate 63.5g, of which sugars 35.1g; Fat 18.4g, of which saturates 11.3g; Cholesterol 46mg; Calcium 62mg; Fibre 1.1g; Sodium 344mg

Yorkshire curd tart

Also known as Yorkshire cheesecake, this tart was originally made with curds made at home from creamy raw milk by adding buttermilk and heating gently. The traditional flavour comes from allspice or "clove pepper". Serve it plain or with cream.

Serves 8

For the pastry

115g/4oz/½ cup butter, diced

225g/8oz/2 cups plain (all-purpose) flour

1 egg yolk

For the filling

large pinch of ground allspice

90g/3½oz/½ cup soft brown sugar

3 eggs, beaten

grated rind and juice of 1 lemon

40g/1½oz/3 tbsp butter, melted

450g/1lb curd (farmer's) cheese

85g/3oz/scant ½ cup raisins or sultanas (golden raisins)

3 To make the filling, mix the allspice with the sugar in a bowl, then stir in the eggs, lemon rind and juice, butter, curd cheese and raisins or sultanas.

4 Pour the filling into the pastry case (pie shell). Bake for about 40 minutes until the filling is lightly set and golden. Serve slightly warm, cut into wedges.

1 Rub the butter into the flour until the mixture resembles fine crumbs. Stir in the egg yolk, with a little water if necessary, and gather the mixture into a smooth ball of dough.

2 On a floured surface, roll out the pastry and use to line a 20cm/8in fluted loose-bottomed flan tin (quiche pan). Chill for 15 minutes. Preheat the oven to 190°C/375°F/Gas 5.

Energy 480kcal/2005kJ; Protein 16.2g; Carbohydrate 48.2g, of which sugars 23.7g; Fat 27g, of which saturates 15.8g; Cholesterol 173mg; Calcium 153mg; Fibre 1.2g; Sodium 451mg.

Syrup sponge pudding

England is famous for its steamed puddings and this one is a classic. The light sponge with its golden coat of syrup brings back memories of childhood when, for many, syrup sponge pudding (probably in a more stodgy version) was one of the highlights of school dinners. Serve this one with freshly made custard or cold pouring cream.

Serves 4–6

45ml/3 tbsp golden (light corn) syrup

115g/4oz/8 tbsp soft butter

115g/4oz/½ cup caster (superfine) sugar

2 eggs

5ml/1 tsp finely grated lemon rind

175g/6oz/1½ cups self-raising (self-rising) flour

30ml/2 tbsp milk

1 Butter a 1.2 litre/2 pint/5 cup heatproof bowl and spoon the golden syrup into the bottom of it.

2 In a large bowl, beat the butter and sugar until pale, light and fluffy.

3 In a separate bowl, beat the eggs and then gradually beat them into the butter-and-sugar mixture together with the lemon rind.

Variations Replace the golden syrup with orange or lemon marmalade, or jam such as raspberry or plum.
• Add a few drops of vanilla extract to the sponge mixture in place of the lemon rind.

4 Sift the flour over the mixture and fold it in lightly using a metal spoon. Gently stir in the milk to give a soft dropping consistency.

5 Spoon the sponge mixture over the golden syrup in the bowl.

6 Cover the pudding with a sheet of greaseproof (waxed) paper or baking parchment, making a pleat in the centre to give the pudding room to rise. Cover this with a large sheet of foil (again pleated in the centre).

7 Tie a length of string securely around the bowl, under the lip, to hold the foil and paper in place.

8 Half-fill a large pan with water and bring it to the boil. Place an inverted saucer or trivet in the bottom and stand the bowl on it. Cover the pan and steam the pudding for about 1½ hours, topping up the pan with more boiling water if necessary.

9 Remove the pudding from the steamer and leave it standing for about 5 minutes before turning out on to a warm plate to serve.

Cook's tips To cook the pudding in the microwave, cover the bowl with baking parchment (but do not tie it on) and cook on medium (500–600W) for 6–8 minutes until the sponge is just cooked through. Leave to stand for 5 minutes before serving.
• The pudding can also be baked for a dryer, cakier texture. Preheat the oven to 190°C/375°F/Gas 5. Cover the bowl with buttered foil and cook for 35–40 minutes. Meanwhile, heat 45ml/3tbsp golden syrup gently with 30ml/2tbsp water. Pour this hot sauce into a jug (pitcher) and serve alongside the pudding for pouring over.

Energy 480kcal/2005kJ; Protein 16.2g; Carbohydrate 48.2g, of which sugars 23.7g; Fat 27g, of which saturates 15.8g; Cholesterol 173mg; Calcium 153mg; Fibre 1.2g; Sodium 451mg

Jam roly poly

This warming winter pudding, with its nursery-sounding name, first appeared on English tables in the 1800s. A savoury version, known as Plough Pudding had a filling of bacon, onion and sage, and was eaten by Victorian stable lads for their supper on chilly days. While boiling is the traditional cooking method for jam roly poly, baking produces a lovely crisp golden crust and a sticky jam filling. Serve it thickly sliced with custard.

Serves 4–6

175g/6oz/1½ cups self-raising (self-rising) flour

pinch of salt

75g/3oz shredded suet (or vegetarian equivalent)

finely grated rind of 1 small lemon

90ml/6 tbsp jam

1 Preheat the oven to 180°C/350°F/ Gas 4 and line a baking sheet with baking parchment.

2 Sift the flour and salt into a bowl and stir in the suet and lemon rind. With a round-ended knife, stir in just enough cold water to enable you to gather the mixture into a ball of soft dough, finishing off with your fingers.

3 Remove the ball of dough from the bowl, and on a lightly floured work surface or board, knead it very lightly until smooth.

Cook's tip For the lightest suet pastry, use as little cold water as possible to mix the dough, and handle it as gently and lightly as you can.

4 Gently roll out the pastry into a rectangle that measures approximately 30 x 20cm/12 x 8in.

5 Using a palette knife or metal spatula, spread the jam evenly over the pastry, leaving the side edges and ends clear.

6 Brush the edges of the pastry with a little water and, starting at one of the short ends, carefully roll up the pastry. Try to keep the roll fairly loose so that the jam is not squeezed out.

7 Place the roll, seam side down, on the prepared baking sheet. Put into the hot oven and cook for 30–40 minutes until risen, golden brown and cooked through. Leave the pudding to cool for a few minutes before cutting into thick slices to serve.

Variation To make a similar traditional nursery favourite, Spotted Dick, replace half the flour with 115g/4oz/2 cups fresh white breadcrumbs; add 50g/2oz/½ cup caster (superfine) sugar and 175g/6oz/¾ cup currants to the flour in step 2. Instead of water to mix, use about 75ml/5 tbsp milk. Leave out the jam and just form into a sausage shape without rolling.

To boil the roly poly
1 Shape the mixture into a roll and wrap loosely (to allow room for the pudding to rise) first in baking parchment and then in a large sheet of foil. Twist the ends of the paper and foil to seal them securely and tie a string handle from one end to the other.

2 Lower the package into a wide pan of boiling water on the stove, cover and boil for about 1½ hours. Check the water level occasionally and top up with boiling water if necessary.

Energy 240kcal/1008kJ; Protein 2.8g; Carbohydrate 33.7g, of which sugars 10.7g; Fat 11.3g, of which saturates 5.7g; Cholesterol 0mg; Calcium 104mg; Fibre 0.9g; Sodium 111mg

Eve's pudding

The name "Mother Eve's pudding", from the biblical Eve, was first used in the 19th century for a boiled suet pudding filled with apples, from which this lighter sponge version developed.

Serves 4–6

115g/4oz/½ cup butter

115g/4oz/½ cup caster (superfine) sugar

2 eggs, beaten

grated rind and juice of 1 lemon

90g/3¼oz/scant 1 cup self-raising (self-rising) flour

40g/1½oz/⅓ cup ground almonds

115g/4oz/scant ½ cup brown sugar

550–675g/1¼–1½lb cooking apples, cored and thinly sliced

25g/1oz/¼ cup flaked (sliced) almonds

1 Preheat the oven to 180°C/350°F/ Gas 4. Beat together the butter and caster sugar in a large mixing bowl until the mixture is very light and fluffy.

2 Gradually beat the eggs into the butter mixture, beating well after each addition, then fold in the lemon rind, flour and ground almonds.

3 Mix the brown sugar, apples and lemon juice and tip the mixture into an ovenproof dish, spreading it out evenly.

4 Spoon the sponge mixture over the top in an even layer and right to the edges. Sprinkle the almonds over. Put into the hot oven and cook for 40–45 minutes until risen and golden brown.

Energy 507kcal/2128kJ; Protein 6.9g; Carbohydrate 65.5g, of which sugars 52.7g; Fat 26.1g, of which saturates 12g; Cholesterol 114mg; Calcium 91mg; Fibre 2.8g; Sodium 159mg

Yorkshire lemon surprise

During cooking a tangy lemon sauce collects beneath a light sponge topping. It's important to bake this dish when it is standing in the bath of hot water, otherwise it will not work.

Serves 4

50g/2oz/¼ cup butter, plus extra for greasing

grated rind and juice of 2 lemons

115g/4oz/½ cup caster (superfine) sugar

2 eggs, separated

50g/2oz/½ cup self-raising (self-rising) flour

300ml/½ pint/1¼ cups milk

1 Preheat the oven to 190°C/375°F/ Gas 5. Use a little butter to grease a 1.2 litre/2 pint/5 cup ovenproof dish.

2 Beat the remaining butter, lemon rind and caster sugar in a bowl until pale and fluffy. Add the egg yolks and flour and beat together well. Gradually whisk in the lemon juice and milk (the mixture may curdle horribly, but don't be alarmed). In a clean bowl, whisk the egg whites until they form stiff peaks.

3 Fold the egg whites lightly into the lemon mixture using a metal spoon, then pour into the prepared dish.

4 Place the dish in a roasting pan pour in hot water to fill halfway up the sides, put into the hot oven and cook for 45 minutes until golden.

Energy 319kcal/1341kJ; Protein 7g; Carbohydrate 43.1g, of which sugars 33.8g; Fat 14.5g, of which saturates 8.1g; Cholesterol 126mg; Calcium 166mg; Fibre 0.4g; Sodium 190mg

Apple and blackberry crumble

The origins of crumble are unclear. It did not appear in recipe books until the 20th century, but has become a firm favourite all over the country. Autumn heralds the harvest of apples and their perfect partners, blackberries. The oatmeal adds even more delicious crunch.

Serves 6–8

115g/4oz/½ cup butter

115g/4oz/1 cup wholemeal (whole-wheat) flour

50g/2oz/½ cup fine or medium oatmeal

50g/2oz/¼ cup soft light brown sugar

a little grated lemon rind (optional)

900g/2lb cooking apples

450g/1lb/4 cups blackberries

squeeze of lemon juice

175g/6oz/scant 1 cup caster (superfine) sugar

1 Preheat the oven to 200°C/400°F/ Gas 6. To make the crumble, rub the butter into the flour, and then add the oatmeal and brown sugar and continue to rub in until the mixture begins to stick together, forming large crumbs.

2 Mix in the grated lemon rind if using. Peel and core the cooking apples and slice into wedges.

3 Put the apples, blackberries, lemon juice, 30ml/2 tbsp water and caster sugar in a shallow ovenproof dish, about 2 litres/3½ pints/9 cups capacity.

4 Cover the fruit with the crumble topping. Put into the hot oven and cook for 15 minutes, then reduce the heat to 190°C/375°F/Gas 5 and cook for 15–20 minutes until golden brown.

Energy 336kcal/1413kJ; Protein 4g; Carbohydrate 53.1g, of which sugars 30.8g; Fat 13.4g, of which saturates 6.8g; Cholesterol 27mg; Calcium 72mg; Fibre 3g; Sodium 81mg

Winter fruit crumble

This crumble uses pears and dried fruit in its base, making it ideal for the winter months. Serve it with custard or whipped cream. At other times of the year, try gooseberries or rhubarb flavoured with orange zest. The almond topping adds a delicious rich texture.

Serves 6

175g/6oz/1½ cups plain (all-purpose) flour

50g/2oz/½ cup ground almonds

175g/6oz/¾ cup butter, diced

115g/4oz/½ cup soft light brown sugar

40g/1½oz flaked (sliced) almonds

1 orange

about 16 ready-to-eat dried apricots

4 firm ripe pears

1 Preheat the oven to 190°C/375°F/ Gas 5. To make the topping, sift the flour into a bowl and stir in the ground almonds. Add the butter and rub it into the flour until the mixture resembles rough breadcrumbs. Stir in 75g/3oz/ ⅓ cup sugar and the flaked almonds.

2 Finely grate 5ml/1 tsp rind from the orange and squeeze out its juice. Halve the apricots and put them into a shallow ovenproof dish. Peel the pears, remove their cores and cut the fruit into small pieces. Scatter the pears over the apricots. Stir the orange rind into the orange juice and sprinkle over the fruit. Scatter the remaining brown sugar over the top.

3 Cover the fruit completely with the crumble mixture and smooth over. Put into the hot oven and cook for about 40 minutes until the topping is golden brown and the fruit is soft (test with the point of a sharp knife).

Energy 615kcal/2569kJ; Protein 9.4g; Carbohydrate 65.7g, of which sugars 42.9g; Fat 36.7g, of which saturates 16.2g; Cholesterol 62mg; Calcium 150mg; Fibre 6.6g; Sodium 190mg

Bread and butter pudding

Plates of white bread and butter were for many years a standard feature of an English tea or nursery supper, and frugal cooks needed to come up with ways to use up the leftovers. Bread and butter pudding was a family favourite until, surprisingly, in the late 20th century it was given a makeover using cream and brioche and began to appear on the menus of upmarket restaurants. This is the original version, which traditionalists prefer.

Serves 4–6

50g/2oz/4 tbsp soft butter

about 6 large slices of day-old white bread

50g/2oz dried fruit, such as raisins, sultanas (golden raisins) or chopped dried apricots

40g/1½oz/3 tbsp caster (superfine) sugar

2 large eggs

600ml/1 pint/2½ cups full cream (whole) milk

1 Preheat the oven to 160°C/325°F/ Gas 5. Lightly butter a 1.2 litre/2 pint/5 cup ovenproof dish.

2 Butter the slices of bread and cut them into small triangles or squares.

3 Arrange half the bread pieces, buttered side up, in the prepared dish and sprinkle the dried fruit and half of the sugar over the top.

4 Lay the remaining bread slices, again buttered side up, evenly on top of the fruit. Sprinkle the remaining sugar evenly over the top.

5 Beat the eggs lightly together, just to break up the yolks and whites, and stir in the milk.

6 Strain the egg mixture and pour it over the bread in the dish. Push the top slices down into the liquid if necessary so that it is evenly absorbed.

7 Leave the pudding to stand for 30 minutes to allow the bread to soak up all the liquid (this is an important step so don't be tempted to skip it).

8 Put the dish into the hot oven and cook for about 45 minutes or until the custard is set and the top is crisp and golden brown. Serve the pudding immediately with pouring cream.

Variation To make a special occasion chocolate bread and butter pudding, complete steps 1–4, omitting the dried fruit if you wish. Break 150g/5oz dark (bittersweet) chocolate into 500ml/17fl oz/generous 2 cups milk and heat gently (on the stove or on low power in the microwave) until the milk is warm and the chocolate has melted. Stir frequently during heating and do not allow the milk to boil. Stir the warm chocolate milk into the beaten eggs in step 5, and then continue with the remaining steps.
• You could replace the dried fruit in either version of the pudding with slices of fresh banana.

Energy 622kcal/2597kJ; Protein 10.5g; Carbohydrate 55.6g, of which sugars 37.8g; Fat 39g, of which saturates 23g; Cholesterol 186mg; Calcium 203mg; Fibre 1.6g; Sodium 350mg

Baked rice pudding

Rice pudding can be traced back to medieval England, when rice and sugar were expensive imports. Much later it was recommended for nursing mothers, gained a reputation as an aphrodisiac and, most enduringly, became a nursery favourite, served with a dollop of jam.

Serves 4

50g/2oz/4 tbsp butter, diced, plus extra for greasing

50g/2oz/¼ cup pudding rice

30ml/2 tbsp soft light brown sugar

900ml/1½ pints/3¾ cups milk

small strip of lemon rind

freshly grated nutmeg

Variations Add some sultanas (golden raisins), raisins or ready-to-eat dried apricots and cinnamon to the pudding.
• Serve with fresh fruit such as sliced peaches, raspberries or strawberries.

1 Preheat the oven to 150°C/300°F/ Gas 2. Butter a 1.2 litre/2 pint/5 cup shallow ovenproof dish.

2 Put the rice, sugar and butter into the dish and stir in the milk. Add the strip of lemon rind and sprinkle a little nutmeg over the surface. Put the pudding into the hot oven.

3 Cook the pudding for about 2 hours, stirring after 30 minutes and another couple of times during the next 1½, hours, until the rice is tender and the pudding is thick and creamy.

4 If you prefer skin on top, leave the pudding undisturbed for the final 30 minutes, or stir again. Serve with jam.

Energy 298kcal/1252kJ; Protein 8.8g; Carbohydrate 54.3g, of which sugars 21.5g; Fat 5.2g, of which saturates 1.4g; Cholesterol 143mg; Calcium 71mg; Fibre 0g; Sodium 185mg

Kentish cherry batter pudding

The south of England was already famous for its cherry orchards in the 16th century. Pink and white cherry blossom heralded the arrival of spring, and Kent was dubbed the "garden of England". The cherry season is short, and puddings like this help to make the most of it.

Serves 4

45ml/3 tbsp cherry brandy or kirsch (optional)

450g/1lb dark cherries, pitted

50g/2oz/½ cup plain (all-purpose) flour

50g/2oz/4 tbsp caster (superfine) sugar, plus extra to serve

2 eggs, separated

300ml/½ pint/¼ cups milk

75g/3oz/5 tbsp butter, melted

1 Sprinkle the cherry brandy or kirsch, if using, over the cherries and leave to soak for about 30 minutes.

2 Stir the flour and sugar together in a mixing bowl, then slowly stir in the egg yolks and milk to make a smooth batter. Stir half the melted butter into the mixture and leave it to rest for 30 minutes.

3 Preheat the oven to 220°C/425°F/ Gas 7. Pour the remaining melted butter over the bottom of a 600ml/ 1 pint/2½ cup ovenproof dish and put it in the oven to heat up.

4 Stiffly whisk the egg whites and fold into the batter with the cherries. Pour into the dish, and bake for 15 minutes. Reduce the heat to 180°C/350°F/Gas 4 and cook for 20 minutes until golden and set. Serve sprinkled with sugar.

Energy 357kcal/1493kJ; Protein 8.1g; Carbohydrate 39.4g, of which sugars 29.8g; Fat 19.7g, of which saturates 11.4g; Cholesterol 140mg; Calcium 147mg; Fibre 1.4g; Sodium 183mg

Baked apples with mincemeat

This quintessential British fruit was once thought to have magical powers and, to this day, apples are linked with many English traditions and festivals. Here, they are baked in the oven with a filling of sweetened dried fruit. They are best served straight from the oven, while still puffed up and before they begin to crumple. Serve with custard or cream.

Serves 4

25g/1oz/2 tbsp butter, plus extra for greasing

4 cooking apples

about 60ml/4 tbsp mincemeat

30ml/2 tbsp honey

1 Preheat the oven to 180°C/350°F/Gas 4. Butter a shallow ovenproof dish.

Variation Replace the mincemeat with chopped dried apricots or dates.

2 With an apple corer or a small sharp knife, remove the cores from the apples. Run a sharp knife around the middle of each apple, cutting through the skin but not deep into the flesh. Stand the apples in the dish.

3 Fill the hollow centres of the apples with mincemeat. Drizzle the honey over the top and dot with butter. Add 60ml/4 tbsp water to the dish. Bake for about 45 minutes until soft throughout, and serve at once.

Energy 70kcal/301kJ; Protein 0.7g; Carbohydrate 17.4g, of which sugars 17.4g; Fat 0.3g, of which saturates 0g; Cholesterol 0mg; Calcium 30mg; Fibre 2.4g; Sodium 9mg

Poached spiced pears

At one time in the history of England, pears were considered by some to be poisonous. Today, the country grows several varieties, particularly in the south-east, East Anglia and the West Midlands. Serve this lightly spiced dish warm or cold, with cream and perhaps some crisp, sweet biscuits for a contrast in texture.

Serves 4

115g/4oz/½ cup caster (superfine) sugar

grated rind and juice of 1 lemon

2.5ml/½ tsp ground ginger

1 small cinnamon stick

2 whole cloves

4 firm ripe pears

Variations Omit the spices and instead flavour the water with ginger or elderflower cordial.
• Use white wine in place of water.

1 Put the sugar in a pan with 300ml/ ½ pint/1½ cups water, the lemon rind and juice, ginger and spices. Heat, stirring, until the sugar has dissolved.

2 Peel the pears, cut them in half lengthways and remove their cores.

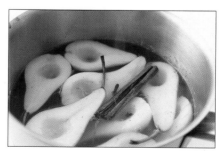

3 Add the pear halves to the pan and bring just to the boil. Cover and simmer gently for about 5 minutes or until the pears are tender, turning them over in the syrup occasionally during cooking. Remove from the heat and leave to cool in the syrup before serving.

Energy 93kcal/392kJ; Protein 0.5g; Carbohydrate 23.6g, of which sugars 23.6g; Fat 0.2g, of which saturates 0g; Cholesterol 0mg; Calcium 17mg; Fibre 3.3g; Sodium 6mg

Summer pudding

This stunning dessert is an essential part of the English summer and it is deceptively simple to make. Use a mixture of fresh seasonal soft fruits and a good quality loaf of white bread. Serve the pudding cold with lashings of thick cream or yogurt.

2 Place all the fruit in a pan with the sugar. Do not add any water. Cook very gently for 4–5 minutes until the juices begin to run.

3 Allow the mixture to cool then spoon the berries, and enough of their juices to moisten the fruit, into the bread-lined bowl. Reserve any remaining juice to serve with the pudding.

4 Fold over the excess bread, then cover the fruit with the remaining slices, trimming to fit. Place a small plate or saucer that fits inside the bowl directly on top of the pudding. Weight it down with a 900g/2lb weight, if you have one, or use a couple of full food cans.

5 Chill the pudding in the refrigerator for at least 8 hours or overnight. To serve, run a knife between the pudding and the bowl and turn out onto a plate. Spoon any reserved juices over the top, and serve with cream or yogurt.

Serves 4–6

about 8 x 1cm/½in-thick slices of day-old white bread, with crusts removed

800g/1¾lb/6–7 cups mixed berries, such as strawberries, raspberries, blackcurrants, redcurrants and blueberries

50g/2oz/¼ cup golden caster (superfine) sugar

lightly whipped double (heavy) cream or thick yogurt, to serve

1 Trim a slice of bread to fit neatly in the base of a 1.2 litre/2 pint/5 cup bowl, then trim another 5–6 slices to line the sides, making sure the bread stands up above the rim.

Energy 192kcal/815kJ; Protein 5.2g; Carbohydrate 43.1g, of which sugars 22.1g; Fat 1g, of which saturates 0g; Cholesterol 0mg; Calcium 82mg; Fibre 2.5g; Sodium 245mg

Devonshire junket

Junkets, or Curds, were eaten by the medieval nobility and became universally popular in Tudor England. The name comes from a Norman word, *jonquette*, meaning cream cheese. Junket is also known as Damask Cream, perhaps because of its smooth, silky consistency.

Serves 4

600ml/1 pint/2½ cups milk

45ml/3 tbsp caster (superfine) sugar

several drops of triple-strength rosewater

10ml/2 tsp rennet

60ml/4 tbsp double (heavy) cream

sugared rose petals, to decorate (optional)

1 Gently heat the milk with 30ml/2 tbsp of the sugar, stirring, until the sugar has dissolved and the temperature reaches body heat (37°C/98.4°F).

2 Remove from the heat and stir in rosewater to taste, then the rennet.

Cook's tip You must use fresh milk for Junket, it will not set properly if homogenized or UHT milk is used. Whole milk gives a better flavour.

3 Pour the junket into serving dishes and leave undisturbed at room temperature for 2–3 hours, until set. Do not move it during this time, otherwise it will separate into curds and whey.

4 Stir the remaining sugar into the cream, then carefully spoon the mixture over the surface of the set junket. Decorate with sugared rose petals, if you wish.

Energy 196kcal/824kJ; Protein 7.5g; Carbohydrate 19.1g, of which sugars 19.1g; Fat 10.6g, of which saturates 6.6g; Cholesterol 29mg; Calcium 193mg; Fibre 0g; Sodium 69mg

Fruit and wine jelly

In 17th-century England, when making jelly was a lengthy process that involved the boiling of calf's hoof, hartshorn or isinglass, it was a centrepiece at high-class banquets. Though jelly now tends to be associated with children's parties it can still make a light and elegant dessert. You need to allow plenty of time for sieving the fruit and cooling the jelly.

Serves 6

600g/1lb 6oz fresh raspberries

140g/5oz/¾ cup white sugar

300ml/½ pint/1¼ cups medium-dry white wine

5 sheets of gelatine (6 if the jelly is to be set in a mould and turned out)

Cook's tip Instead of making your own fruit juice, use a carton of juice, such as mango, cranberry or orange, sweetened to taste.

1 Put the raspberries and sugar in a pan with 100ml/3½fl oz/scant ½ cup water and heat gently until the fruit releases its juices and becomes very soft, and the sugar has dissolved.

2 Remove the pan from the heat, tip the mixture into a fine nylon sieve (strainer) or jelly bag over a large bowl, and leave to strain – this will take some time but do not squeeze the fruit or the resulting juice may be cloudy.

3 When the juice from the fruit has drained into the bowl, make it up to 600ml/1 pint/2½ cups with water if necessary. Soak the gelatine in cold water for about 5 minutes to soften it.

4 Heat half the juice until very hot but not quite boiling. Remove from the heat. Squeeze the softened gelatine to remove excess water, then stir it into the hot juice until dissolved. Stir in the remaining raspberry juice and the wine.

5 Pour into stemmed glasses and chill until set. Alternatively, set the jelly in a wetted mould and turn out onto a pretty plate for serving.

Energy 178kcal/758kJ; Protein 8.6g; Carbohydrate 29.3g, of which sugars 29.3g; Fat 0.3g, of which saturates 0.1g; Cholesterol 0mg; Calcium 42mg; Fibre 2.5g; Sodium 6mg.

Almond and rosewater blancmange

In the Middle Ages blancmange (literally "white food") was a banqueting dish that contained chicken and rice as well as almonds and sugar. Later, arrowroot and cornflour were used as thickeners (and indeed are often still used). During Victoria's reign the dessert began to be set with gelatine in fancy moulds and became very fashionable.

Serves 6

5 sheets of gelatine

1 lemon

450ml/¾ pint/1⅔ cups milk

115g/4oz/½ cup caster (superfine) sugar

450ml/¾ pint/scant 2 cups single (light) cream

85g/3oz/¾ cup ground almonds

about 2.5ml/1 tsp triple-strength rosewater

fresh or sugared rose petals, to decorate (optional)

1 Soak the gelatine leaves in cold water for about 5 minutes to soften them.

2 Thinly pare strips of rind from the lemon, taking care not to include the white pith. Heat the milk gently with the lemon rind until it just comes to the boil. Discard the rind.

Variations Omit the lemon rind and add 2.5ml/1 tsp vanilla extract at step 3.
• Instead of rosewater, use your favourite liqueur.

3 Lift the softened sheets of gelatine out of the soaking water, squeezing out the excess. Stir the gelatine into the hot milk until dissolved. Stir in the sugar until it has dissolved. Add the cream, almonds and rosewater to taste and mix well.

4 Pour into one large or six individual wetted moulds, put into the refrigerator and chill until completely set.

5 Turn the blancmange out of its mould(s) just before serving. Decorate with rose petals if you wish.

Energy 350kcal/1462kJ; Protein 10.2g; Carbohydrate 26.2g, of which sugars 25.8g; Fat 23.5g, of which saturates 10.6g; Cholesterol 46mg; Calcium 201mg; Fibre 1.1g; Sodium 57mg

Fruit trifle

Everyone's favourite, trifle is a classic English dessert. The earliest trifles were creamy confections rather like fools, but in the 18th century the dish took the form familiar today, with layers of sponge soaked in wine or sherry, topped with syllabub or whipped cream.

Serves 6–8

1 x 15–18cm/6–7in plain sponge cake

225g/8oz/¾ cup raspberry jam

150ml/¼ pint/⅔ cup medium or sweet sherry

450g/1lb ripe fruit, such as pears and bananas, peeled and sliced

300ml/½ pint/1¼ cups whipping cream

toasted flaked (sliced) almonds, to decorate or glacé (candied) cherries and angelica, (optional)

For the custard

450ml/¾ pint/scant 2 cups full cream (whole) milk

1 vanilla pod (bean)

3 eggs

25g/1oz/2 tbsp caster (superfine) sugar

1 To make the custard, put the milk into a pan with the vanilla pod, split along its length, and bring almost to the boil. Remove from the heat. Leave to cool a little while you whisk the eggs and sugar together lightly. Remove the vanilla pod from the milk and gradually whisk the milk into the egg mixture.

2 Rinse out the pan with cold water and return the mixture to it. (Alternatively, use a double boiler, or a bowl over a pan of boiling water.)

3 Stir over a low heat until it thickens enough to coat the back of a wooden spoon; do not allow the custard to boil. Turn the custard into a bowl, cover and set aside while you assemble the trifle.

4 Halve the sponge cake horizontally, spread with the raspberry jam and sandwich together. Cut into slices and use to line the bottom and lower sides of a large glass serving bowl.

Variation The sherry could be replaced with fruit juice, whisky or a fruit liqueur.

5 Sprinkle the sponge cake with the sherry. Spread the fruit over the sponge in an even layer. Pour the custard on top, cover with clear film (plastic wrap) to prevent a skin forming, and leave to cool and set. Chill until required.

6 To serve, whip the cream and spread it over the custard. Decorate with the almonds, cherries and angelica, if using.

Energy 631kcal/2615kJ; Protein 8.4g; Carbohydrate 24.9g, of which sugars 18.4g; Fat 53.1g, of which saturates 28.4g; Cholesterol 258mg; Calcium 155mg; Fibre 1.4g; Sodium 116mg

Gooseberry and elderflower fool

Little can be simpler than swirling cooked fresh fruit into whipped cream. Rhubarb is another favourite seasonal flavour to use in this recipe. Be sure to serve fool in pretty glasses or dishes, accompanied by crisp biscuits to add a contrast of texture.

Serves 4

500g/1¼lb gooseberries

300ml/½ pint/1¼ cups double (heavy) cream

about 115g/4oz/1 cup icing (confectioners') sugar, to taste

30ml/2 tbsp elderflower cordial

mint sprigs, to decorate

crisp biscuits (cookies), to serve

1 Place the gooseberries in a heavy saucepan, cover and cook over a low heat, shaking the pan occasionally, until tender. Tip the gooseberries into a bowl, crush them with a fork or potato masher, then leave to cool completely.

2 Whip the cream until soft peaks form, then fold in half the crushed fruit. Add sugar and elderflower cordial to taste. Sweeten the remaining fruit to taste.

3 Layer the cream mixture and the crushed gooseberries in four dessert dishes or tall glasses, then cover and chill until ready to serve. Decorate the fool with mint sprigs and serve with crisp sweet biscuits.

Variations When elderflowers are in season, cook 2–3 elderflower heads with the gooseberries and omit the elderflower cordial.
• For rhubarb fool use squeezed orange juice in place of elderflower cordial.

Energy 366kcal/1521kJ; Protein 3.5g; Carbohydrate 24.2g, of which sugars 21.8g; Fat 28.4g, of which saturates 16.7g; Cholesterol 70mg; Calcium 111mg; Fibre 1.9g; Sodium 41mg

Eton mess

The "mess" consists of whipped cream, crushed meringue and sliced or mashed strawberries, all mixed together before serving. This pudding gets its name from the famous public school, Eton College, where it is served at the annual picnic on 4 June.

Serves 4

450g/1lb ripe strawberries

45ml/3 tbsp elderflower cordial or orange liqueur

300ml/½ pint/1¼ cups double (heavy) cream

4 meringues or meringue baskets

Cook's tips Serve Eton mess just as it is or accompanied by crisp sweet biscuits (cookies).
• Make the dish with other soft fruit, such as lightly crushed raspberries or blackcurrants.
• This is a useful recipe to know if you are trying to make a large meringue and it cracks, as you can just break it up completely and serve it this way.

1 Remove the green hulls from the strawberries and slice the fruit into a bowl, reserving a few for decoration.

2 Sprinkle with the elderflower cordial or fruit liqueur. Cover the bowl and chill for about 2 hours.

3 Whip the cream until soft peaks form. Crush the meringue into small pieces. Add the fruit and most of the meringue to the cream and fold in lightly. Spoon into serving dishes and chill until required. Before serving, decorate with the reserved strawberries and meringue.

Energy 526kcal/2182kJ; Protein 3.5g; Carbohydrate 32.8g, of which sugars 32.8g; Fat 40.4g, of which saturates 25.1g; Cholesterol 103mg; Calcium 60mg; Fibre 1.4g; Sodium 53mg

Syllabub

This dish can be traced back to the 17th century, when it is said to have been made by pouring fresh milk, straight from the cow, on to spiced cider or ale, creating a frothy foam. Later, cream and wine were used to make an impressive and luxurious dessert.

Serves 6

1 orange

65g/2½oz/⅓ cup caster (superfine) sugar

60ml/4 tbsp medium dry sherry

300ml/½ pint/1¼ cups double (heavy) cream

strips of crystallized orange, to decorate

sponge fingers or crisp biscuits (cookies) to serve

1 Finely grate 2.5ml/½ tsp rind from the orange, then squeeze out its juice.

2 Put the orange rind and juice, sugar and sherry into a large bowl and stir until the sugar is completely dissolved. Stir in the cream. Whip the mixture until thick and soft peaks form.

3 Spoon the syllabub into wine glasses.

4 Chill the glasses of syllabub until ready to serve, then decorate with strips of crystallized orange. Serve with sponge fingers or crisp biscuits.

Cook's Tips Syllabub is lovely spooned over a bowl of fresh soft fruit such as strawberries, apricots, raspberries or blackberries.
• Add a pinch of ground cinnamon to the mixture in step 2.

Energy 310kcal/1282kJ; Protein 1.1g; Carbohydrate 14.5g, of which sugars 14.5g; Fat 26.9g, of which saturates 16.7g; Cholesterol 69mg; Calcium 41mg; Fibre 0.3g; Sodium 15mg

Teatime Treats

Afternoon tea became an English ritual in the 19th century and is still served in many homes, hotels and tea shops. It can be a simple affair or an elaborate spread and an opportunity to use the best china. So a pot of tea may be accompanied by scones or cake; or there may be a selection of teas with an array of savoury and sweet goodies – sandwiches, scones, tarts, cakes and biscuits.

Anchovy toast

The Victorians loved anchovies in all kinds of dishes. In the late 19th century it became fashionable to serve anchovy butter in the French style – spread on fried bread and topped with Cornish clotted cream – but simple toast fingers are more suited to modern tastes.

Serves 4–6

50g/2oz can of anchovy fillets in olive oil, well drained

75g/3oz/6 tbsp soft unsalted butter

15ml/1 tbsp finely chopped fresh parsley

generous squeeze of lemon juice

ground black pepper

4–6 slices of bread

1 Using a mortar and pestle, crush the anchovies to make a thick paste. Add the butter, parsley and lemon juice and mix well, seasoning to taste with black pepper. (Alternatively, put all the ingredients into a food processor and blend to a smooth paste.) Cover and chill until required.

2 Just before serving, toast the bread on both sides. Spread the anchovy butter on the hot toast, cut into fingers and serve immediately.

Sausage rolls

Small sausage rolls rank high in the league of popular teatime and party foods. They are delicious when homemade, particularly if quality butcher's sausagemeat is used to fill them. Serve them hot or cold. They also make an ideal addition to a picnic or packed lunch.

Makes about 16

175g/6oz/1½ cups plain (all-purpose) flour

pinch of salt

40g/1½oz/3 tbsp lard, diced

40g/1½oz/3 tbsp butter, diced

250g/9oz pork sausagemeat (bulk sausage)

beaten egg, to glaze

1 To make the pastry, sift the flour and salt and add the lard and butter. Rub the fats into the flour until the mixture resembles fine crumbs. Stir in about 45ml/3 tbsp cold water until the mixture can be gathered into a smooth ball of dough. Wrap and chill for 30 minutes.

2 Preheat the oven to 190°C/375°F/ Gas 5. Roll out the pastry on a lightly floured surface to make a rectangle about 30cm/12in long. Cut lengthways into two long strips.

3 Divide the sausagemeat into two pieces and, on a lightly floured surface, shape each into a long roll the same length as the pastry. Lay a roll on each strip of pastry. Brush the pastry edges with water and fold them over the meat, pressing the edges together to seal them well.

4 Turn the rolls over and, with the seam side down, brush with beaten egg. Cut each roll into eight and place on a baking sheet. Bake in the hot oven for 30 minutes until crisp and golden brown. Cool on a wire rack.

Energy 159kcal/661kJ; Protein 4g; Carbohydrate 10.4g, of which sugars 0.7g; Fat 11.5g, of which saturates 6.7g; Cholesterol 32mg; Calcium 55mg; Fibre 0.4g; Sodium 512mg

Energy 125kcal/521kJ; Protein 2.5g; Carbohydrate 10.3g, of which sugars 0.5g; Fat 8.4g, of which saturates 3.9g; Cholesterol 14mg; Calcium 23mg; Fibre 0.4g; Sodium 142mg

Cheese straws

Cheese-flavoured pastries became popular when it was customary (for gentlemen, particularly) to eat a small savoury at the end of a long, sophisticated meal. Now we are more likely to eat cheese straws as an appetizer with pre-dinner drinks.

Makes about 10

75g/3oz/⅔ cup plain (all-purpose) flour

40g/1½oz/3 tbsp butter, diced

40g/1½oz mature hard cheese, such as Cheddar, finely grated

1 egg

5ml/1 tsp ready-made mustard

salt and ground black pepper

1 Preheat the oven to 180°C/350°F/ Gas 4. Line a baking sheet with baking parchment.

2 Sift the flour and seasoning and add the butter. Rub the butter into the flour until the mixture resembles fine crumbs. Stir in the cheese.

3 Lightly beat the egg with the mustard. Add half the egg to the flour, stirring in until the mixture can be gathered into a smooth ball of dough.

4 Roll the dough out to make a square measuring about 15cm/6in. Cut into ten lengths. Place on the baking sheet and brush with the remaining egg. Put into the hot oven and cook for about 12 minutes until golden brown. Transfer to a wire rack and serve warm.

Cucumber sandwiches

Think of Edwardian England and invariably afternoon tea with dainty cucumber sandwiches come to mind. Cucumbers were first grown in English hothouses in the 16th century, just waiting for the sandwich to be invented two hundred years later.

Serves 4

½ cucumber

soft unsalted butter

8 slices of white bread

salt and ground black pepper

1 Peel the cucumber and cut it into thin slices. Sprinkle with salt, place in a colander and leave for about 20 minutes to drain. Butter the slices of bread on one side. Lay the cucumber over four slices of bread and sprinkle with pepper.

2 Top with the remaining bread. Press down lightly and trim off the crusts

3 Cut the sandwiches into squares, fingers or triangles. Serve immediately.

Energy 49kcal/206kJ; Protein 1.5g; Carbohydrate 3.9g, of which sugars 0.1g; Fat 3.1g, of which saturates 1.9g; Cholesterol 13mg; Calcium 32mg; Fibre 0.2g; Sodium 39mg

Energy 174kcal/735kJ; Protein 6.8g; Carbohydrate 29.2g, of which sugars 3.3g; Fat 4.2g, of which saturates 1.1g; Cholesterol 5mg; Calcium 92mg; Fibre 1g; Sodium 307mg

Scones with jam and cream

For most people, English afternoon tea without a plate of scones would be unthinkable.
They are equally good served with cream and soft fruit, such as strawberries or raspberries.
It's important that they are freshly baked, but they are quick and easy to make.

Makes about 12

450g/1lb/4 cups self-raising (self-rising) flour, or 450g/1lb/4 cups plain (all-purpose) flour and 10ml/2 tsp baking powder

5ml/1 tsp salt

55g/2oz/¼ cup butter, chilled and cut into small cubes

15ml/1 tbsp lemon juice

about 400ml/14fl oz/1⅔ cups milk, plus extra to glaze

jam and cream, to serve

1 Preheat the oven to 230°C/450°F/Gas 8. Sift the flour, baking powder (if using) and salt into a mixing bowl, and stir to mix through.

2 Add the butter and rub it lightly into the flour with your fingertips until the mixture resembles fine, even-textured breadcrumbs.

3 Whisk the lemon juice into the milk and leave for about 1 minute to thicken slightly, then pour into the flour mixture and mix quickly to make a soft but pliable dough. The softer the mixture, the lighter the resulting scones will be, but if it is too sticky they will spread during baking and lose their shape.

4 Knead the dough briefly, then roll it out on a lightly floured surface to a thickness of at least 2.5cm/1in.

5 Using a 5cm/2in biscuit (cookie) cutter, and dipping it into flour each time, stamp out 12 rounds. Place the dough rounds on a well-floured baking sheet. Re-roll the trimmings and cut out more scones.

6 Brush the tops of the scones with a little milk then put into the hot oven and cook for about 20 minutes, or until risen and golden brown.

7 Remove from the oven and wrap the scones in a clean dish towel to keep them warm and soft until ready to eat. Eat the scones with plenty of jam and a generous dollop of clotted or whipped double cream.

Variation To make savoury cheese scones, add 115g/4oz/1 cup of grated cheese (preferably mature Cheddar or another strong hard cheese) to the dough and knead it in thoroughly before rolling out and cutting into shapes. Cheese scones make a good accompaniment to soup.

Energy 177kcal/749kJ; Protein 4.7g; Carbohydrate 30.7g, of which sugars 2.2g; Fat 4.8g, of which saturates 2.8g; Cholesterol 12mg; Calcium 93mg; Fibre 1.2g; Sodium 43mg

Crumpets

Toasting crumpets in front of an open fire became particularly popular during the reign of Queen Victoria. They are made with a yeast batter, cooked in metal rings on a griddle. Serve them freshly toasted and spread with butter and maybe a drizzle of golden syrup.

Makes about 10

225g/8oz/2 cups plain (all-purpose) flour

2.5ml/½ tsp salt

2.5ml/½ tsp bicarbonate of soda (baking soda)

5ml/1 tsp fast-action yeast granules

150ml/¼ pint/⅔ cup milk

oil, for greasing

1 Sift the flour, salt and bicarbonate of soda into a bowl and stir in the yeast. Make a well in the centre. Heat the milk with 200ml/7fl oz/scant 1 cup water until lukewarm and tip into the well.

2 Mix well with a whisk or wooden spoon, beating vigorously to make a thick smooth batter. Cover and leave in a warm place for about 1 hour until the mixture has a spongy texture.

3 Heat a griddle or heavy frying pan. Lightly oil the hot surface and the inside of three or four metal rings, each measuring about 8cm/3½in in diameter. Place the oiled rings on the hot surface and leave for 1–2 minutes until hot.

4 Spoon the batter into the rings to a depth of about 1cm/½in. Cook over a medium-high heat for about 6 minutes until the top surface is set and bubbles have burst open to make holes.

5 When set, carefully lift off the metal rings and flip the crumpets over, cooking the second side for just 1 minute until lightly browned.

6 Lift off and leave to cool completely on a wire rack. Repeat with the remaining crumpet mixture. Just before serving, toast the crumpets on both sides and butter generously.

Energy 93kcal/393kJ; Protein 3g; Carbohydrate 16.5g, of which sugars 1g; Fat 2.1g, of which saturates 1g; Cholesterol 21mg; Calcium 48mg; Fibre 0.6g; Sodium 21mg

Drop scones

Thin, light and spongy, drop scones are also known as girdlecakes, griddlecakes and Scotch pancakes. They can be served hot or cold with butter and honey, syrup or jam. They are good with whipped cream and fresh soft fruit too.

3 Make a well in the centre of the flour mixture, then stir in the egg. Stir in the milk a little at a time, adding enough to give a thick creamy consistency.

4 Cook in batches. Drop three or four even spoonfuls of the mixture, spaced slightly apart, on the griddle or frying pan. Cook over a medium heat for 2–3 minutes, until bubbles rise to the surface and burst.

5 Turn the scones over and cook for a further 2–3 minutes on the other side, until golden underneath. Place the cooked scones between the folds of a clean dish towel while cooking the remaining batter. Serve warm, with butter and honey.

Cook's tip Placing the freshly cooked drop scones in a clean folded dish towel keeps them soft, warm and moist. Serve them like this and invite your guests to help themselves.

Makes 8–10

115g/4oz/1 cup plain (all-purpose) flour

5ml/1 tsp bicarbonate of soda (baking soda)

5ml/1 tsp cream of tartar

25g/1oz/2 tbsp butter, cut into small cubes

1 egg, beaten

about 150ml/¼ pint/⅔ cup milk

butter and clear honey, to serve

1 Sift the flour, bicarbonate of soda and cream of tartar into a mixing bowl. Rub the butter into the flour until the mixture resembles fine breadcrumbs.

2 Lightly grease a griddle pan or heavy frying pan, and heat it.

Energy 60kcal/252kJ; Protein 2g; Carbohydrate 11.1g, of which sugars 1.8g; Fat 1.1g, of which saturates 0.2g; Cholesterol 11mg; Calcium 66mg; Fibre 0.4g; Sodium 56mg

Newcastle singin' hinnies

In Tyneside, "hinny" is a term of endearment for friends or children, but these hinnies are thin, scone-like little cakes and "singin'" refers to the sound they make as they cook on the hot buttered griddle. Serve them warm, split and spread with butter.

Makes about 20

400g/14 oz/3½ cups self-raising (self-rising) flour

7.5ml/1½ tsp baking powder

5ml/1 tsp salt

50g/2oz butter, diced, plus extra for greasing

50g/2oz lard, diced

50g/2oz/¼ cup caster (superfine) sugar

75g/3oz/⅓ cup currants, raisins or sultanas (golden raisins)

about 150ml/¼ pint/⅔ cup milk

3 Transfer to a lightly floured surface and roll out to about 5mm/¼in thick. With a 7.5cm/3in cutter, cut into rounds, gathering up the offcuts and re-rolling to make more.

4 Heat a heavy frying pan or griddle. Rub with butter and cook the scones in batches for 3–4 minutes on each side until well browned. Lift off and keep warm until all are cooked.

1 Sift the flour, baking powder and salt into a large bowl. Add the butter and lard and, with your fingertips, rub them into the flour until the mixture resembles fine breadcrumbs.

2 Stir in the sugar and dried fruit. Add the milk and, with a flat-ended knife, stir the mixture until it can be gathered into a ball of soft dough.

Variation Instead of making small cakes, try cooking the dough in a large, pan-sized circle, cutting it into wedges first to facilitate easy turning.

Energy 132kcal/557kJ; Protein 2.3g; Carbohydrate 21.1g, of which sugars 5.8g; Fat 4.9g, of which saturates 2.4g; Cholesterol 8mg; Calcium 42mg; Fibre 0.7g; Sodium 118mg

Shropshire soul cakes

These little cakes were served on All Souls' Day (2 November), when it was customary to go "souling" or singing prayers for the dead. In return, the singers received a soul cake. The original recipe would have included plain flour but self-raising produces a lighter result.

Makes about 20

450g/1lb/4 cups self-raising (self-rising) flour

5ml/1 tsp ground mixed (apple pie) spice

2.5ml/½ tsp ground ginger

175g/6oz/¾ cup soft butter

175g/6oz/¾ cup caster (superfine) sugar, plus extra for sprinkling

2 eggs, lightly beaten

50g/2oz/¼ cup currants, raisins or sultanas (golden raisins)

about 30ml/2 tbsp milk

1 Preheat the oven to 180°C/350°F/ Gas 4. Lightly grease two baking sheets or line with baking parchment. Sift the flour and spices into a bowl, and set aside. In a large bowl, beat the butter with the sugar until the mixture is light, pale and fluffy.

2 Gradually beat the eggs into the mixture. Fold in the flour mixture and the dried fruit, then add sufficient warm milk to bind the mixture and gather it up into a ball of soft dough.

3 Transfer to a lightly floured surface and roll out to about 5mm/¼in thick. With a floured 7.5cm/3in cutter, cut into rounds, gathering up the offcuts and re-rolling to make more.

4 Arrange the cakes on the prepared baking sheets. Prick the surface of the cakes lightly with a fork then, with the back of a knife, mark a deep cross on top of each.

5 Put the cakes into the hot oven and cook for about 15 minutes until risen and golden brown.

6 Sprinkle the cooked cakes with a little caster sugar and then transfer to a wire rack to cool.

Energy 191kcal/803kJ; Protein 2.9g; Carbohydrate 28.4g, of which sugars 11.3g; Fat 8.1g, of which saturates 4.8g; Cholesterol 38mg; Calcium 45mg; Fibre 0.7g; Sodium 62mg

Cornish saffron bread

This was originally made at Easter. Its beautiful yellow colour and distinctive flavour come from saffron, a precious spice from western Asia that was possibly introduced to Cornwall by Phoenicians trading in Cornish tin. Serve sliced, spread with Cornish butter.

Makes 1 loaf

good pinch of saffron threads

450g/1lb/4 cups plain (all-purpose) flour

2.5ml/½ tsp salt

50g/2oz/4 tbsp butter, diced

50g/2oz/4 tbsp lard, diced

10ml/2 tsp fast-action yeast granules

50g/2oz caster (superfine) sugar

115g/4oz/½ cup currants, raisins or sultanas (golden raisins), or a mixture

50g/2oz chopped mixed candied peel

150ml/¼ pint/⅔ cup milk

beaten egg, to glaze

1 Put the saffron in a bowl and add 150ml/¼ pint/⅔ cup boiling water. Cover and leave for several hours to allow the colour and flavour to develop.

2 Sift the flour and salt into a large bowl. Add the butter and lard and rub them into the flour until the mixture resembles fine breadcrumbs. Stir in the yeast granules, sugar, dried fruit and chopped m ixed peel. Make a well in the centre.

3 Add the milk to the saffron water and warm to body heat. Tip the liquid into the flour and stir until it can be gathered into a ball. Cover with oiled plastic wrap and leave in a warm place for about 1 hour, until doubled in size.

4 Grease and line a 900g/2lb loaf tin (pan) with baking parchment. Turn the dough on to a lightly floured surface and knead gently and briefly.

5 Put the dough in the prepared tin, cover and leave in a warm place for 30 minutes until nearly doubled in size. Preheat the oven to 200°C/400°F/Gas 6.

5 Brush the top of the loaf with beaten egg and cook for 40 minutes or until risen and cooked through; cover with foil if it starts to brown too much. Leave in the tin for about 15 minutes before turning out onto a wire rack to cool.

Energy 3041kcal/12821kJ; Protein 50.7g; Carbohydrate 516.8g, of which sugars 173.9g; Fat 99.9g, of which saturates 48.7g; Cholesterol 162mg; Calcium 1018mg; Fibre 18.5g; Sodium 541mg

Lincolnshire plum bread

This bread, always shaped into small loaves, is particularly associated with Christmas. It is sweet and rich and is eaten with cheese, sliced and buttered or toasted like rich teacake.

Makes 2 small loaves

450g/1lb/4 cups strong white bread flour

pinch of salt

5ml/1 tsp ground cinnamon

5ml/1 tsp freshly grated nutmeg

12.5ml/2½ tsp fast-action yeast granules

60ml/4 tbsp soft light brown sugar

115g/4oz/8 tbsp butter, diced

about 100ml/3½fl oz/scant ½ cup milk

2 eggs, lightly beaten

225g/8oz/1 cup mixed dried fruit, such as currants, raisins and chopped mixed (candied) peel

1 Sift together the flour, salt and spices and stir in the yeast and sugar. Gently heat the butter and milk until just melted. Add the eggs to the flour and mix well until the mixture can be gathered into a smooth ball of dough. Cover with oiled cling film (plastic wrap) and leave in a warm place for about 1 hour until doubled in size. Grease and line two 450g/1lb loaf tins (pans) with baking parchment and preheat the oven to 190°C/375°F/Gas 5.

2 Knead the dough briefly on a lightly floured surface, working in the dried fruit evenly. Divide between the prepared tins, cover with oiled cling film and leave in a warm place for 30 minutes, or until nearly doubled in size.

3 Cook the loaves for 40 minutes, then turn them out of their tins and return to the hot oven for about 5 minutes or until they sound hollow when tapped on the base. Cool on a wire rack.

Energy 1710kcal/7211kJ; Protein 32.2g; Carbohydrate 285.2g, of which sugars 113.7g; Fat 57.1g, of which saturates 32.5g; Cholesterol 316mg; Calcium 535mg; Fibre 9.1g; Sodium 465mg

Marmalade teabread

A cake that's perfect for serving with a cup of tea, this is especially popular in the north-west of England. The marmalade gives it a lovely flavour, at the same time keeping it moist.

Makes 8–10 slices

200g/7oz/1¾ cups plain (all-purpose) flour

5ml/1 tsp baking powder

6.25ml/1¼ tsp ground cinnamon

100g/3½oz/7 tbsp butter, cut into small pieces

55g/2oz/3 tbsp soft light brown sugar

1 egg

60ml/4 tbsp chunky orange marmalade

about 45ml/3 tbsp milk

60ml/4 tbsp glacé icing, to decorate

shreds of orange and lemon rind, to decorate

1 Preheat the oven to 160°C/325°F/ Gas 3. Grease a 450g/1lb loaf tin (pan), and line with baking parchment.

2 Sift the flour, baking powder and cinnamon together, then add the butter and rub in with the fingertips until the mixture resembles fine crumbs. Stir in the sugar.

3 Beat the egg lightly in a small bowl and mix it with the marmalade and most of the milk.

4 Mix the milk mixture into the flour mixture, adding more milk if necessary to give a soft dropping consistency.

5 Transfer the mixture to the prepared tin, put into the hot oven and cook for about 1¼ hours, until the cake is firm to the touch and cooked through.

6 Leave the cake to cool for 5 minutes, then turn on to a wire rack. Carefully peel off the lining paper and leave the cake to cool completely.

7 Drizzle the glacé icing over the top of the cake and decorate with shreds of orange and lemon rind.

Energy 250kcal/1049kJ; Protein 3.5g; Carbohydrate 38g, of which sugars 19g; Fat 10.4g, of which saturates 6.2g; Cholesterol 48mg; Calcium 56mg; Fibre 0.8g; Sodium 86mg

Victoria sponge

This light cake was named in honour of Queen Victoria. Often referred to as a Victoria sandwich, it is based on equal quantities of fat, sugar, eggs and flour. It has come to be regarded as the classic English cake and remains a favourite for baking competitions.

Serves 6–8

3 large eggs

few drops of vanilla extract

175g/6oz/¾ cup soft butter

175g/6oz/¾ cup caster (superfine) sugar

175g/6oz/1½ cups self-raising (self-rising) flour

about 60ml/4 tbsp jam

icing (confectioner's) sugar, to dust

1 Preheat the oven to 180°C/350°F/ Gas 4. Butter two 20cm/8in sandwich tins (layer pans) and line the bases of each with baking parchment.

2 Lightly beat the eggs with the vanilla extract. In a large mixing bowl, whisk the butter with the sugar until the mixture is pale, light and fluffy.

3 Gradually add the eggs, beating well after each addition. Sift the flour over the top and, using a metal spoon, fold in lightly until the mixture is smooth.

4 Divide the mixture between the prepared tins. Cook for 20 minutes until golden and firm to the touch.

5 Leave the cakes to cool in the tins for a few minutes then carefully turn out on to a wire rack. Remove the paper and leave to cool completely.

6 When the cakes are cold, sandwich the two halves together with plenty of jam. Finally, sift a little icing sugar over the top.

Variations Instead of vanilla extract, beat a little finely grated lemon zest into the butter and sugar mixture in step 2. Sandwich the cakes halves together with lemon curd.
• For a cream cake, sandwich with a thin layer of strawberry jam and a thick layer of whipped cream, topped with sliced fresh strawberries. Decorate the top of the cake with whipped cream and extra strawberries.

Energy 368kcal/1543kJ; Protein 4.6g; Carbohydrate 44.7g, of which sugars 28.5g; Fat 20.3g, of which saturates 12g; Cholesterol 118mg; Calcium 104mg; Fibre 0.7g; Sodium 241mg

Chocolate cake (2 cakes)

The first chocolate arrived in England in the 1500s, and the 17th century saw the opening of expensive chocolate houses, which were frequented by the rich and famous. Today, chocolate cake is a staple of every self-respecting tea table in England.

Serves 10–12

225g/8oz/2 cups plain (all-purpose) flour

5ml/1 tsp bicarbonate of soda (baking soda)

50g/2oz/½ cup (unsweetened) cocoa powder

125g/4½oz/9 tbsp soft butter

250g/9oz/1¼ cups caster (superfine) sugar

3 eggs, beaten

250ml/8fl oz/1 cup buttermilk

For the chocolate buttercream

175g/6oz/1½ cups icing (confectioner's) sugar

115g/4oz/½ cup soft unsalted butter

few drops of vanilla extract

50g/2oz dark chocolate

1 Butter two 20cm/8in sandwich tins (pans) and line the bases with baking parchment. Preheat the oven to 180°C/350°F/Gas 4. Sift the flour with the bicarbonate of soda and cocoa.

2 Beat the butter and sugar until light and fluffy. Gradually beat in the eggs. Add the flour and buttermilk, mix well.

3 Spoon into the prepared tins. Place into the hot oven and cook for 30–35 minutes until firm to the touch. Turn out of the tins, peel off the paper and leave on a wire rack to cool completely.

4 To make the chocolate buttercream, sift the icing sugar into a bowl. In a separate bowl, beat the butter until very soft and creamy.

5 Beat in half the sifted icing sugar until smooth and light. Gradually beat in the remaining sugar and the vanilla extract. Break the chocolate into squares. Melt in a bowl over a pan of hot water or in a microwave oven on low.

6 Mix the melted chocolate into the buttercream. Use half to sandwich the cakes together, and the rest on the top.

Energy 430kcal/1790kJ; Protein 7.8g; Carbohydrate 29.5g, of which sugars 28.8g; Fat 32.1g, of which saturates 13.6g; Cholesterol 96mg; Calcium 92mg; Fibre 1.9g; Sodium 125mg

Almond and raspberry swiss roll

This light and airy whisked sponge cake is rolled up with a rich and mouthwatering filling
of fresh raspberries and cream, making a perfect treat for tea in the garden in summer.
It is also be delicious filled with other soft fruits, such as strawberries or blackcurrants.

4 Sprinkle a sheet of baking parchment liberally with caster sugar. Turn out the cake onto the paper, and leave to cool with the tin still in place.

5 Lift the tin off the cooled cake and carefully peel away the lining paper from the base of the cake.

6 Whip the cream until it holds its shape. Fold in 250g/8oz/1¼ cups of the raspberries, and spread over the cooled cake, leaving a narrow border.

Serves 8

butter, for greasing

150g/5oz/1¼ cups plain (all-purpose) flour

4 eggs

115g/4oz/½ cup caster (superfine) sugar, plus extra for sprinkling

25g/1oz/2 tbsp ground almonds

225ml/8fl oz/1 cup double (heavy) cream

275g/10oz/1½ cups fresh raspberries

flaked (sliced) almonds, to decorate

1 Preheat the oven to 200°C/400°F/ Gas 6. Grease a 33 x 23cm/13 x 9in Swiss roll tin (jelly roll pan) and line with baking parchment, cut to fit. Sift the flour and set aside.

2 Beat the eggs and sugar with an electric mixer for about 10 minutes until the mixture is thick and pale. Sift the pre-sifted flour over the mixture and gently fold in with a metal spoon, together with the ground almonds.

3 Spoon the mixture into the prepared tin and bake for 10–12 minutes, until the sponge is well risen and springy to the touch.

7 Carefully roll up the cake from a narrow end, using the paper to lift the sponge. Sprinkle with caster sugar. Serve decorated with the remaining raspberries and toasted flaked almonds.

Cook's tip This is a cake that needs to be eaten straight away, as cream and fresh fruit do not keep. Fill with raspberry jam or lemon curd instead of cream if you want it to last longer.

Energy 271kcal/1127kJ; Protein 4.7g; Carbohydrate 16.7g, of which sugars 11.9g; Fat 21.1g, of which saturates 11.2g; Cholesterol 114mg; Calcium 56mg; Fibre 1.2g; Sodium 35mg

Honey cake

The earliest form of sweetener, honey has been an important ingredient in cooking throughout history, and there have been lots of different recipes baked through the centuries. Its flavour changes subtly according to the type of honey used.

Makes 16 squares

175g/6oz/¾ cup butter

175g/6oz/¾ cup clear honey

115g/4oz/½ cup soft brown sugar

2 eggs, lightly beaten

15–30ml/1–2 tbsp milk

225g/8oz/2 cups self-raising (self-rising) flour

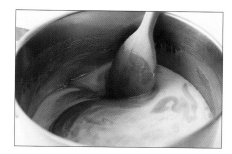

3 Beat the eggs and milk into the cooled mixture. Sift the flour over the top, stir in and beat well until smooth.

4 Tip the mixture into the prepared tin, levelling the surface. Put into the hot oven and cook for about 30 minutes until well risen, golden brown and firm to the touch.

5 Leave the cake to cool in the tin for 20 minutes then turn out, leaving the lining paper in place, onto a wire rack and leave to cool completely.

6 Peel off the paper and cut the cake into 16 squares.

1 Grease and line a 23cm/9in square cake tin (pan) with baking parchment. Preheat the oven to 180°C/350°F/Gas 4.

2 Gently heat the butter, honey and sugar, stirring frequently until well amalgamated. Set aside and leave to cool slightly.

Variation Add 5ml/1tsp ground cinnamon or grated nutmeg to the flour in step 3.

Energy 152kcal/639kJ; Protein 1.9g; Carbohydrate 23.5g, of which sugars 13g; Fat 6.3g, of which saturates 3.8g; Cholesterol 26mg; Calcium 30mg; Fibre 0.4g; Sodium 49mg

Christmas cake

Rich cakes need at least a month to mature, so Christmas cake is best made by about Hallowe'en. The same recipe can be used for a wedding cake. It may be finished in the traditional way with almond paste and white icing, or topped with glazed fruit and nuts.

Makes 1 x 20cm/8in round or 18cm/7in square cake

225g/8oz/2 cups plain (all-purpose) flour

pinch of salt

7.5ml/1½ tsp mixed (apple pie) spice

900g/2lb/5 cups mixed dried fruit

50g/2oz/½ cup slivered almonds

115g/4oz/⅔ cup glacé (candied) cherries, halved

115g/4oz/⅔ cup chopped mixed (candied) peel

225g/8oz/1 cup soft butter

225g/8oz/1 cup soft dark brown sugar

15ml/1 tbsp black treacle (molasses)

finely grated rind of 1 orange

5ml/1 tsp vanilla extract

4 large eggs

150ml/¼ pint/⅔ cup whisky or brandy

1 Line a 20cm/8in round or 18cm/7in square loose-based cake tin (pan) with three layers of greased baking parchment, extending 5cm/2in over the top of the tin. Tie a thick band of folded brown paper around the outside. Preheat the oven to 160°C/325°F/Gas 3.

2 Sift the flour, salt and spice. Put the dried fruit in a large bowl with the almonds, cherries and mixed peel and stir in 15ml/1 tbsp of the flour.

3 In another bowl, beat the butter and sugar until light and fluffy, then add the treacle, orange rind and vanilla extract.

4 Add the eggs, one at a time, adding a little of the flour mixture with each egg and beating well after each addition. Fold in the fruit, remaining flour and 30ml/2 tbsp of the whisky or brandy.

5 Put the mixture into the prepared tin, levelling with the back of a spoon and making a slight hollow in the centre. Place the cake in the centre of the hot oven and cook for about 1½ hours, or until just beginning to brown.

6 Reduce the heat to 150°C/300°F/Gas 2 and cook for another 3 hours until cooked. Protect the top of the cake from over-browning by covering loosely with foil or brown paper.

7 When cooked, the top of the cake will feel springy to the touch and a skewer pushed into the centre will come out clean. Leave to cool completely, then remove the lining papers and turn the cake upside down.

8 Using a skewer, make small holes all over the base of the cake and sprinkle over the remaining whisky or brandy. (Repeat this procedure after a week if you wish.)

9 Wrap the cake in a double layer of baking parchment followed by a thick layer of foil. Store in an airtight tin in a cool place. Just before Christmas add your chosen decoration.

Energy 8145kcal/34415kJ; Protein 74.4g; Carbohydrate 1528.9g, of which sugars 1385.8g; Fat 204.6g, of which saturates 105.4g; Cholesterol 1154mg; Calcium 1859mg; Fibre 38.1g; Sodium 2326mg

Simnel cake

This cake dates back to medieval times, and is traditionally served at Easter, the marzipan balls on top represent the 11 faithful apostles. It is also sometimes made for Mothering Sunday, when the almond paste top is decorated with fresh or crystallized spring flowers.

Makes 1 x 18cm/7in round cake

175g/6oz/¾ cup butter

175g/6oz/scant 1 cup soft brown sugar

3 large eggs, beaten

225g/8oz/2 cups plain (all-purpose) flour

2.5ml/½ tsp ground cinnamon

2.5ml/½ tsp freshly grated nutmeg

150g/5oz/1 cup each of currants, sultanas (golden raisins) and raisins

85g/3oz/generous ½ cup glacé (candied) cherries, quartered

85g/3oz/generous ½ cup mixed (candied) peel, chopped

grated rind of 1 large lemon

450g/1lb almond paste

1 egg white, lightly beaten

1 Grease and line an 18cm/7in round cake tin (pan) and tie a double layer of brown paper round the outside.

2 Beat the butter and sugar until pale and fluffy, then gradually beat in the eggs. Lightly fold in the flour, spices, dried fruits, cherries, mixed peel and lemon rind.

3 Preheat the oven to 160°C/325°F/Gas 3. Roll half the almond paste to a 16cm/6½in circle on a surface dusted with caster sugar.

4 Spoon half the cake mixture into the prepared tin and place the circle of almond paste on top of the mixture. Spoon the remaining cake mixture on top and level the surface.

5 Put the cake into the hot oven and cook for 1 hour. Reduce the oven temperature to 150°C/300°F/Gas 2 and cook for another 2 hours. Leave to cool for 1 hour in the tin, then turn out and cool on a wire rack.

6 Brush the cake with egg white. Roll out half the remaining almond paste to a 28cm/11in circle and cover the cake. Roll the remaining paste into 11 balls and attach with egg white. Brush the top of the cake with more egg white and grill (broil) until lightly browned.

Energy 8108kcal/34162kJ; Protein 104g; Carbohydrate 1323.3g, of which sugars 1113.8g; Fat 303.9g, of which saturates 132.5g; Cholesterol 1442mg; Calcium 1557mg; Fibre 33.4g; Sodium 2080mg

West country apple cake

The sweet-acid flavour of this fruity cake is refreshing, and cooking apples produce a very moist cake, though you can use eating apples if you prefer for a sweeter result.

Makes 1 x 18cm/7in round cake

225g/8oz cooking apples, peeled, cored and chopped

juice of ½ lemon

225g/8oz/2 cups plain (all-purpose) flour

7.5ml/1½ tsp baking powder

115g/4oz/½ cup butter, cut into small pieces

165g/5½oz/scant 1 cup soft light brown sugar

1 egg, beaten

about 30–45ml/2–3 tbsp milk

2.5ml/½ tsp ground cinnamon

1 Grease and line an 18cm/7in round cake tin (pan) with baking parchment. Preheat the oven to 180°C/350°F/Gas 4.

2 Toss the apples with the lemon juice. Sift the flour and baking powder. Rub in the butter until the mixture resembles fine crumbs. Stir in 115g/4oz/¾ cup of the sugar, the apples and the egg.

3 Add enough milk to give a soft dropping consistency. Transfer to the prepared tin. Mix together the remaining sugar and the cinnamon and sprinkle over the cake mixture. Put into the hot oven and cook for 45–50 minutes, until firm to the touch. Leave to cool in the tin for 10 minutes, then transfer to a wire rack to cool.

Energy 3810kcal/16031kJ; Protein 35.7g; Carbohydrate 596.6g, of which sugars 451.9g; Fat 159g, of which saturates 68.4g; Cholesterol 260mg; Calcium 617mg; Fibre 16.4g; Sodium 839mg

Yorkshire parkin

This moist ginger cake is traditionally served cut into squares. In former days, when a quantity of parkin was being baked, one batch was sometimes eaten hot with apple sauce.

Makes 16–20 squares

300ml/½ pint/1¼ cups milk

225g/8oz/1 cup golden (corn) syrup

225g/8oz/¾ cup black treacle (molasses)

115g/4oz/½ cup butter

50g/2oz/scant ¼ cup dark brown sugar

450g/1lb/4 cups plain (all-purpose) flour

2.5ml/½ tsp bicarbonate of soda (baking soda)

7.5ml/1½ tsp ground ginger

350g/12oz/4 cups medium oatmeal

1 egg, beaten

icing (confectioner's) sugar, to dust

1 Preheat the oven to 180°C/350°F/Gas 4. Gently heat together the milk, syrup, treacle, butter and sugar, stirring until smooth; do not boil. Grease a 20cm/8in square cake tin (pan) and line the base and sides with baking parchment.

Cook's tip The flavour and texture of the cake improves if it is wrapped in foil and stored in an airtight container for several days.

2 Sieve the flour into a bowl, add the bicarbonate of soda, ginger and oatmeal. Make a well in the centre and add the egg, then the warmed mixture, stirring to make a smooth batter.

3 Pour the batter into the tin and bake for about 45 minutes, until firm to the touch. Cool slightly in the tin, then turn out onto a wire rack to cool completely. Cut into squares and dust with icing sugar.

Energy 273kcal/1152kJ; Protein 5.3g; Carbohydrate 50g, of which sugars 20.1g; Fat 7.1g, of which saturates 3.3g; Cholesterol 23mg; Calcium 127mg; Fibre 1.9g; Sodium 102mg

Brandy snaps with cream

Records show that brandy snaps were sold at fairs in the north of England in the 19th century. They were considered a special treat for high days and holidays. Every kitchen had a little pot of ground ginger ready for adding to cakes, biscuits and these lacy wafer rolls.

Makes about 12

50g/2oz/4 tbsp butter

50g/2oz/¼ cup caster (superfine) sugar

30ml/2 tbsp golden (corn) syrup

50g/2oz/½ cup plain (all-purpose) flour

2.5ml/½ tsp ground ginger

5ml/1 tsp brandy

150ml/¼ pint/⅔ cup double (heavy) or whipping cream

1 Preheat the oven to 180°C/350°F/ Gas 4. Line two or three baking (cookie) sheets with baking parchment.

2 Gently heat the butter, sugar and golden syrup (in a saucepan on the hob or in the microwave on low power) until the butter has melted and the sugar has dissolved.

3 Remove the pan from the heat. Sift the flour and ginger and stir into the mixture with the brandy.

4 Put small spoonfuls of the mixture on the lined baking sheets, spacing them about 10cm/4in apart to allow for spreading. Put into the hot oven and cook for 7–8 minutes or until bubbling and golden. Meanwhile, grease the handles of several wooden spoons.

5 Allow the wafers to cool on the tin for about 1 minute then loosen with a palette knife and quickly roll around the spoon handles. Leave to set for 1 minute, before sliding them off the handles and cooling completely on a wire rack.

6 Just before serving, whip the cream until soft peaks form, spoon into a piping bag and pipe a little into both ends of each brandy snap.

Cook's tip Store unfilled brandy snaps in an airtight container, where they should stay crisp for up to one week. Fill with cream just before serving.

Energy 121kcal/505kJ; Protein 0.6g; Carbohydrate 11.7g, of which sugars 10g; Fat 7.9g, of which saturates 5g; Cholesterol 21mg; Calcium 16mg; Fibre 0.1g; Sodium 24mg

Suffolk buns

Caraway seeds were once a popular ingredient of breads, cakes and sweet confections, and were often chewed to sweeten the breath. Farmers traditionally gave seed cakes and buns to their labourers at the end of wheat sowing, particularly in the south-east.

Makes about 12

350g/12 oz/3 cups plain (all-purpose) flour

115g/4oz/⅔ cup ground rice or semolina

10ml/2 tsp baking powder

115g/4oz/½ cup butter

75g/3oz/½ cup caster (superfine) sugar, plus extra for sprinkling

30ml/2 tbsp caraway seeds

2 eggs

about 75ml/5 tbsp milk

1 Preheat the oven to 200°C/400°F/ Gas 6. Line a baking sheet with baking parchment. Sift the flour, ground rice and baking powder together into a large mixing bowl.

2 Add the butter and, with your fingertips, rub it into the flour until the mixture resembles fine breadcrumbs. Stir the sugar and caraway seeds in to the flour mixture.

3 Lightly beat the eggs and stir them into the flour mixture, together with sufficient milk to enable you to gather the mixture into a ball of soft dough. Transfer to a lightly floured surface.

4 Roll out to about 2.5cm/1in thick. Using a 5cm/2in biscuit (cookie) cutter, cut into rounds, gathering up the offcuts and re-rolling to make more.

5 Arrange the rounds on the lined baking sheet, setting them quite close together so they support each other as they rise.

6 Put into the hot oven and cook for 15–20 minutes until risen and golden brown. Transfer to a wire rack and dust with caster sugar. Leave to cool.

Cook's tip Replace the caraway seeds with 50g/2oz dried fruit, such as raisins or finely chopped apricots.

Energy 244kcal/1026kJ; Protein 5.1g; Carbohydrate 36.9g, of which sugars 7.3g; Fat 9.5g, of which saturates 5.4g; Cholesterol 53mg; Calcium 60mg; Fibre 1.1g; Sodium 75mg

Maids of honour

These little delicacies were allegedly being enjoyed by Anne Boleyn's maids of honour when Henry VIII first met her in Richmond Palace in Surrey, and he is said to have named them. Originally they would have been made with strained curds, made by adding rennet to milk.

3 Put the curd cheese into a bowl and add the almonds, sugar and lemon rind. Lightly beat the eggs with the butter and add to the cheese mixture. Mix well.

4 Spoon the mixture into the pastry cases. Bake for about 20 minutes, until the pastry is well risen and the filling is puffed up, golden brown and just firm to the touch.

Makes 12

250g/9oz ready-made puff pastry

250g/9oz/1¼ cups curd (farmer's) cheese

60ml/4 tbsp ground almonds

45ml/3 tbsp caster (superfine) sugar

finely grated rind of 1 small lemon

2 eggs

15g/½ oz/1 tbsp butter, melted

icing (confectioner's) sugar, to dust

Variation Sprinkle the filling with a little freshly grated nutmeg at the end of step 4.

1 Preheat the oven to 200°C/400°F/ Gas 6. Grease a 12-hole bun tray.

2 Roll out the puff pastry very thinly on a lightly floured surface and, using a 7.5/3in cutter, cut out 12 circles. Press the pastry circles into the prepared tray and prick well with a fork. Chill while you make the filling.

5 Transfer to a wire rack (the filling will sink down as it cools). Serve warm or at room temperature, dusted with a little sifted icing sugar.

Energy 182kcal/758kJ; Protein 5.2g; Carbohydrate 12.6g, of which sugars 5.1g; Fat 12.9g, of which saturates 3g; Cholesterol 43mg; Calcium 31mg; Fibre 0.4g; Sodium 85mg

Jam tarts

"The Queen of Hearts, she made some tarts, all on a summer's day; the Knave of Hearts, he stole those tarts, and took them quite away!" goes the nursery rhyme. Jam tarts have long been a treat at birthday parties and are often a child's first attempt at baking.

Makes 12

175g/6oz/1½ cups plain (all purpose) flour

pinch of salt

30ml/2 tbsp caster (superfine) sugar

85g/3oz/6 tbsp butter, diced

1 egg, lightly beaten

jam

1 Sift the flour and salt and stir in the sugar. Rub in the butter until the mixture resembles fine crumbs. Stir in the egg and gather into a smooth dough ball.

2 Chill the pastry ball for 30 minutes. Meanwhile, preheat the oven to 220°C/425°F/Gas 7 and lightly grease a 12-hole bun tray.

3 Roll out the pastry on a lightly floured surface to about 3mm/⅛in thick and, using a 7.5/3in fluted biscuit (cookie) cutter, cut out 12 circles. Press the pastry circles into the prepared tray. Put a teaspoonful of jam into each.

4 Put into the hot oven and cook for 15–20 minutes until the pastry is cooked and light golden brown. Carefully lift the tarts on to a wire rack and leave to cool before serving.

Mince pies

These small pies have become synonymous with Christmas. To eat one per day for the 12 days of Christmas was thought to bring happiness for the coming year.

Makes 12

225g/8oz/2 cups plain (all-purpose) flour

pinch of salt

45ml/3 tbsp caster (superfine) sugar, plus extra for dusting

115g/4oz/½ cup butter, diced

1 egg, lightly beaten

about 350g/12oz mincemeat

1 Sift the flour and salt and stir in the sugar. Rub in the butter until the mixture resembles fine crumbs. Stir in the egg and gather into a smooth dough.

2 Chill the pastry for 30 minutes. Meanwhile, preheat the oven to 220°C/425°F/Gas 7 and lightly grease a 12-hole bun tray.

3 Roll out the pastry on a lightly floured surface to about 3mm/⅛in thick and, using a 7.5/3in cutter, cut out 12 circles. Press into the prepared tray. Gather up the offcuts and roll out again, cutting slightly smaller circles to make 12 lids. Spoon mincemeat into each case, dampen the edges and top with a pastry lid. Make a small slit in each pie.

4 Bake for 15–20 minutes until light golden brown. Transfer to a wire rack to cool and serve dusted with sugar.

Energy 114kcal/479kJ; Protein 1.1g; Carbohydrate 18.8g, of which sugars 12.5g; Fat 4.3g, of which saturates 2.6g; Cholesterol 18mg; Calcium 16mg; Fibre 0.3g; Sodium 39mg

Energy 236kcal/993kJ; Protein 2.5g; Carbohydrate 36.7g, of which sugars 22.4g; Fat 9.8g, of which saturates 5.2g; Cholesterol 37mg; Calcium 43mg; Fibre 1g; Sodium 70mg

Yorkshire fat rascals

These delicious teacakes from the north of England are a cross between a scone and a rock cake and are really simple to make. They would originally have been baked in a small pot oven standing over an open fire. Serve them warm or cold, just as they are or with butter.

Makes 10

350g/12oz/3 cups self-raising (self rising) flour

175g/6oz/¾ cup butter, diced

115g/4oz/½ cup caster (superfine) sugar

75g/3oz/⅓ cup mixed currants, raisins and sultanas (golden raisins)

25g/1oz/1½ tbsp chopped mixed peel

50g/2oz/⅓ cup glacé (candied) cherries

50g/2oz/⅓ cup blanched almonds, roughly chopped

1 egg

about 75ml/5 tbsp milk

1 Preheat the oven to 200°C/400°F/ Gas 6. Line a baking sheet with baking parchment.

2 Sift the flour into a large bowl. Add the butter and, with your fingertips, rub it into the flour until the mixture resembles fine breadcrumbs (alternatively whizz the ingredients briefly in a food processor).

3 Stir in the sugar, dried fruit, peel, cherries and almonds.

4 Lightly beat the egg and stir into the flour mixture with sufficient milk to gather the mixture into a ball of dough.

5 With lightly floured hands, divide the dough into ten balls, press them into rough circles about 2cm/¾in thick and arrange on the prepared baking sheet.

6 Cook for 15–20 minutes until risen and golden brown. Transfer to a wire rack to cool.

Energy 375kcal/1574kJ; Protein 5.6g; Carbohydrate 50g, of which sugars 23.2g; Fat 18.4g, of which saturates 9.6g; Cholesterol 57mg; Calcium 93mg; Fibre 1.8g; Sodium 129mg

Ginger snaps

It was once customary to serve ginger snaps and spiced ale on Twelfth Night, the evening of 5 January and a night of parties and practical jokes. Since then, many an English tale has been written over a plate of ginger snaps and a cup of strong tea.

Makes about 24

115g/4oz/½ cup butter, diced

115g/4oz/½ cup caster (superfine) sugar

115g/4oz/½ cup golden (corn) syrup

225g/8oz/2 cups plain (all-purpose) flour

10ml/2 tsp ground ginger

5ml/1 tsp bicarbonate of soda (baking soda)

1 Preheat the oven to 180°C/350°F/ Gas 4. Line two or three baking sheets with baking parchment. Gently heat the butter, sugar and syrup until the butter has melted and the sugar has dissolved. Leave to cool slightly.

2 Sift the flour, ginger and bicarbonate of soda and stir into the mixture in the pan to make a soft dough.

3 Arrange balls of the dough on the prepared baking sheets, well spaced out. Flatten each ball slightly with a palette knife or metal spatula.

Cook's tip Measuring syrup is easier if you dip a metal spoon in very hot water first, then quickly dry it.

4 Put one tray into the hot oven and cook for about 12 minutes until golden brown (take care not to overcook them – they burn easily). Leave to cool on the baking sheet for 1–2 minutes then carefully transfer to a wire rack to crisp up and cool completely while you cook the remaining biscuits.

Energy 101kcal/424kJ; Protein 1g; Carbohydrate 16.1g, of which sugars 9g; Fat 4.1g, of which saturates 2.5g; Cholesterol 10mg; Calcium 17mg; Fibre 0.3g; Sodium 43mg

Oat biscuits

In England oats have been one of the principle crops since the days of the Anglo-Saxons and King Alfred the Great. By the 14th century, the grain had become a major export. Nutritious and delicious, oats are a major ingredient in these biscuits.

3 Sift the flour and stir into the mixture in the pan, together with the oats, to make a soft dough.

4 Roll the dough into small balls and arrange them on the prepared baking sheets, leaving plenty of room for them to spread. Flatten each ball slightly with a palette knife or a metal spatula.

5 Put one tray into the hot oven and cook for 12–15 minutes until golden brown and cooked through.

6 Leave to cool on the baking sheet for 1–2 minutes then carefully transfer to a wire rack to crisp up and cool completely, while you cook the remaining batches.

Makes about 18

115g/4oz/½ cup butter

115g/4oz/½ cup soft brown sugar

115g/4oz/½ cup golden (corn) syrup

150g/5oz/1¼ cups self-raising (self-rising) flour

150g/5oz rolled porridge oats

1 Preheat the oven to 180°C/350°F/Gas 4. Line two or three baking (cookie) sheets with baking parchment, or grease them with butter.

2 Gently heat the butter, sugar and golden syrup until the butter has melted and the sugar has dissolved. Remove from the heat and leave to cool slightly.

Variation Add 25g/1oz/¼ cup finely chopped toasted almonds or walnuts, or a small handful of dried fruit (raisins or sultanas) in step 3.

Energy 151kcal/637kJ; Protein 1.8g; Carbohydrate 23.9g, of which sugars 11.9g; Fat 6g, of which saturates 3.3g; Cholesterol 14mg; Calcium 22mg; Fibre 0.8g; Sodium 59mg

Melting moments

As the name suggests, these crisp biscuits really do melt in the mouth. They have a texture like shortbread but are covered in rolled oats to give a crunchy surface and extra flavour, and traditionally topped with a nugget of glacé cherry.

Makes 16–20

40g/1½oz/3 tbsp soft butter

65g/2½oz/5 tbsp lard

85g/3oz/6 tbsp caster (superfine) sugar

1 egg yolk, beaten

few drops of vanilla or almond extract

150g/5oz/1¼ cups self-raising (self-rising) flour

rolled oats, for coating

4–5 glacé (candied) cherries

3 Spread rolled oats on a sheet of baking parchment and toss the balls in them until evenly coated.

4 Place the balls, spaced slightly apart, on two baking (cookie) sheets. Flatten each ball a little with your thumb. Cut the cherries into quarters and place a piece of cherry on top of each biscuit (cookie). Put into the hot oven and cook for 15–20 minutes, until they are lightly browned.

5 Allow the biscuits to cool for a few minutes on the baking sheets before transferring them to a wire rack to cool completely.

1 Preheat the oven to 180°C/350°F/Gas 4. Beat together the butter, lard and sugar, then gradually beat in the egg yolk and vanilla or almond extract.

2 Sift the flour over and stir to make a soft dough. Roll into 16–20 small balls.

Energy 88kcal/370kJ; Protein 0.7g; Carbohydrate 10.9g, of which sugars 5.4g; Fat 5g, of which saturates 2.4g; Cholesterol 7mg; Calcium 30mg; Fibre 0.3g; Sodium 40mg.

Easter biscuits

These sweet, lightly spiced cookies have fluted edges and are flecked with currants. In the West Country they are also known as Easter cakes rather than biscuits.

Makes 16–18

115g/4oz/½ cup soft butter

85g/3oz/6 tbsp caster (superfine) sugar, plus extra for sprinkling

1 egg

200g/7oz/1¾ cups plain (all-purpose) flour

2.5ml/½ tsp mixed (apple pie) spice

2.5ml/½ tsp ground cinnamon

55g/2oz/scant ½ cup currants

15ml/1 tbsp chopped mixed (candied) peel

15–30ml/1–2 tbsp milk

1 Preheat the oven to 200°C/400°F/ Gas 6. Lightly grease two baking sheets or line with baking parchment.

2 Beat together the butter and sugar until light and fluffy. Separate the egg, reserving the white, and beat the yolk into the mixture.

3 Sift the flour and spices over the mixture, then fold in the currants and peel, adding sufficient milk to make a fairly soft dough.

4 Knead the dough lightly on a floured surface then roll out to 5mm/¼in thick. Cut out circles using a 5cm/2in fluted biscuit (cookie) cutter. Arrange on the sheets and cook for 10 minutes.

5 Beat the egg white and brush gently over the biscuits (cookies). Sprinkle with caster sugar and return to the oven for 10 minutes until golden. Transfer to a wire rack to cool.

Energy 116kcal/485kJ; Protein 1.5g; Carbohydrate 15.4g, of which sugars 7g; Fat 5.7g, of which saturates 3.4g; Cholesterol 24mg; Calcium 25mg; Fibre 0.4g; Sodium 46mg

Shrewsbury cakes

Despite their traditional name, these are crisp, lemony shortbread biscuits with fluted edges, which have been made and sold in the town of Shrewsbury since the 17th century.

3 Sift the flour over the top and add the lemon rind. Stir in and then gather up the mixture to make a stiff dough. Knead the dough lightly on a floured surface then roll it out to about 5mm/¼in thick.

4 Using a 7.5cm/3in fluted biscuit (cookie) cutter, cut out circles and arrange on the baking sheets. Gather up the offcuts and roll out again to make more biscuits.

5 Put into the hot oven and cook for about 15 minutes, until firm to the touch and lightly browned.

6 Transfer to a wire rack and leave to crisp up and cool completely.

Variations Omit the lemon rind and sift 5ml/1 tsp ground mixed (apple pie) spice with the flour in step 3.
• Add 25g/1oz/2 tbsp currants or raisins to the mixture in step 3.

Makes about 20

115g/4oz/½ cup soft butter

140g/5oz/¾ cup caster (superfine) sugar

2 egg yolks

225g/8oz/2 cups plain (all-purpose) flour

finely grated rind of 1 lemon

1 Preheat the oven to 180°C/350°F/ Gas 4. Line two baking sheets with baking parchment.

2 In a mixing bowl, beat the softened butter with the sugar until pale, light and fluffy. Beat in each of the egg yolks one at a time, beating thoroughly after each addition.

Energy 115kcal/482kJ; Protein 1.4g; Carbohydrate 16.1g, of which sugars 7.5g; Fat 5.4g, of which saturates 3.2g; Cholesterol 32mg; Calcium 23mg; Fibre 0.4g; Sodium 37mg

Index

Bibliography

Davidson, Alan. *The Oxford Companion to Food* (Oxford
   University Press, 1999)
Hartley, Dorothy. *Food in England* (Little, Brown and Company,
   1954)
Grigson, Jane. *English Food* (Penguin, 1974)
Mason, Laura with Brown, Catherine. *Traditional Foods of
   Britain* (Prospect Books, 1999)
Making a Meal of It, Two Thousand Years of English Cookery
   (English Heritage, 2005)
Spencer, Colin. *British Food, An Extraordinary Thousand Years of
   History* (Grub Street, 2002)

Author's acknowledgements

The author thanks the following organizations in particular:
www.bbc.co.uk
www.greatbritishkitchen.co.uk

Picture acknowledgements

Bridgeman Picture Library: pp 9 , 10, 11 both, 12 both, 13, 14
both, 15, 29 both, 30 both, 36 bottom.
Corbis: pp 8 both, 28 both, 31 both, 34 bottom, 35 both, 36
top, 37 top right.
iStockphoto: pp 16 top, 17 both, 18, 19 both, 20 both, 21, 22
both, 23 both, 24 both, 25 both, 26, 27 all, 30 top right, 37
top right and bottom.